SUNSHINE
CLINIC

A Novel with Recipes

Book Three

Meera K

March 2025

MEERA EKKANATH KLEIN

Cover Image (iStock.com)
Interior Images (freepik.com)

First Edition 2024 @ Fleets Bay Press

Fleets Bay Press

SUNSHINE
CLINIC

*To Uncle, Aunty, and Alan for their quiet
inspiration and encouragement.
And to Duke for being the best writing companion.
You are missed every day.*

BOOKS BY
MEERA EKKANATH KLEIN

Seeing Ceremony: A Novel with Recipes

My Mother's Kitchen: A Novel with Recipes

PROLOGUE

O n my fifth birthday, my mother gave me a bright yellow raincoat with a matching hat and rubber boots. I've always loved bright colors and wanted to wear the yellow raincoat everywhere. It seemed natural to wear it on my first day of kindergarten. No rain was predicted, but that didn't stop me from slipping into the yellow jacket.

"You will be hot," my older sister, Meena, warned me. "And you look silly."

I stuck my tongue out at her.

"I don't care," I said. "I want to wear it."

My mother tried to change my mind.

"You should save the coat for the first rainy day, Thangam," she said. "Then it will be more special."

I thought about it for a moment.

"No," I said, shaking my head. "I want to wear this coat now."

My mother and sister exchanged looks, but they said nothing more. My mother's farm manager, Bhojan, drove us to school that day. Sitting in the car, I was a little warm but determined to keep the coat on. I wiped my forehead surreptitiously, hoping my sister didn't see me sweating.

The day started off well. All the girls admired my boots and hat. One of them, who would later become my best friend, asked me to join her on the monkey bars. It was easy to swing my way across the first few bars, but then gravity started to work against me, and I found I couldn't hold on to the slippery bars. I let go and fell flat on my back with a thud. The shredded wood chips on the ground broke my fall, and I was stunned momentarily. I looked up to see a stranger staring down at me.

"Hey, little girl," a voice asked. "Are you okay?"

I couldn't speak; the wind was knocked out of me, but I managed to nod.

"Here," the voice continued. "Let me help you up."

Strong fingers twined around mine, pulling me to my feet. I stared at the person who had helped me up. It was a boy. He was taller than me and looked quite different from my other classmates. His skin was pale, and his hair shone with a red-gold hue. He had the bluest eyes I had ever seen. I had only seen such blue eyes on one person in Mahagiri: our Scottish friend, Mac.

"You looked like a big sunny-side-up egg," the boy said. His accent was as different as his looks. "What's your name?"

I seemed to have lost the ability to talk.

A classmate spoke up, "Her name is Thangam."

"Thangam?" the boy with the accent repeated. "Does that mean yellow? Because you are as bright as the sun."

My classmates, who had gathered around us, lost interest in me and wandered off, except for the pale-skinned boy.

"Come on, little Sunny," he said. "Why don't you sit down for a while?"

I followed him to the small wooden bench on the far side of the playground. We sat in silence; the sun was warm on my face, and I was getting hot in my raincoat. Removing it wasn't an option, so I sat still and longed for the famous Mahagiri breeze.

"Can I ask why you are wearing a raincoat? Do you think it will rain?" the boy asked.

I had to concentrate hard to understand his accent. His r's seemed to run into each other. He even sounded a lot like Mac.

I shook my head, no, but still didn't say a word.

We sat silently until the bell rang, and the students all started returning to class. I got up to follow my classmates. The tall boy started to walk away, but he turned around at the edge of the playground and raised a hand. I was too shy to wave back. Instead, I looked down at my yellow rubber boots.

Later that afternoon, when school was let out, I looked for the tall boy but didn't see him. My brother Appu approached me, and we walked to the waiting car.

"I think I want to be called Sunny," I told him.

"Why?"

I shrugged my shoulders and said, "I like the name."

Appu looked at me with serious brown eyes, "It suits you, but maybe that should be your school name."

I smiled and replied, "Yes, Sunny will be my school name."

CHAPTER ONE
COMING HOME

S omeone I know, probably my mother, used to say the best part of leaving is coming home again.

I had to agree as I looked out the slow-moving train's window. I had decided to take the "match-stick train" up the mountain from Pellaur to Mahagiri. It had been over two years since my last and very brief visit. Medical college leaves little time for vacation and family visits.

If you haven't already guessed, my name is Thangam, but now everyone calls me Sunny except my mother.

I was going home to see my mother, Sudha, and older sister Meena. Meena was now married with a daughter. She and her businessman husband, Raj, live in Mahagiri and run a tea room and plantation. The tea room is in the home of our old friend Mac, a Scottish man who had settled in the area over fifty years ago. Before he died nearly ten years ago, Mac had left his house and estate to Meena and her husband.

I grew up in the hilltop town of Mahagiri. When my twin brother Appu and I were nine years old, our father unexpectedly died from a heart attack. My mother was so grief-stricken that she forgot all about us. Meena took care of us with the help of our housekeeper Devi, an elderly cousin whom we called Muthi (granny), and our old nanny Ayah. Ayah and Muthi have since passed away, and Devi oversees the household.

After Meena was married, Appu and I decided we needed a change of scenery and pleaded with our mother to let us attend the out-of-town high school. She agreed, and we became boarders. We were independent for the first time in our short lives, and the distance from home allowed us to mature.

Our old nanny, Ayah, had a reputation as a healer. She had never gone to college but had learned about herbs, tinctures, and medicinal teas from her mentor. I loved to watch her mix dried herbs and make restorative potions as a child. I really wanted to be like Ayah because everyone respected her. Meena was beautiful and bright as the sun, while I was the forgotten younger daughter. No one paid much attention to me. I found solace in books and was smart enough to get into a prestigious medical school. For the last decade, all I did was study. Finally, I was finished with schooling and a grueling internship. Now, I am a qualified doctor. I was coming home to relax and figure out my next career move.

Usually, our family drove from Pellaur to Mahagiri. Still, I've always liked to travel by the miniature train, popular with tourists. My sister used to call this train a "toy match-stick train," and there was something playful about the miniature train. It was painted a cheery bright blue and yellow. The conductor and en-gineer wore old-fashioned pin-striped railway uniforms. It was comforting in an antiquated way.

As it chugged and puffed its way up the steep hillside, I was reminded of the children's story "The Little Engine That Could," I silently encouraged the tiny engine to keep climbing.

I leaned out the window to take in the breathtaking view of the deep canyon. In the distance, I could see the deep red-orange blossoms of the Flame of the Forest tree. A few daring young tourists were leaning out of their windows. I had no death wish and sat down to watch the train slowly pass a magnificent waterfall. With the slight breeze, I could feel drops of moisture land on my bare arms.

As we climbed up the mountain, the air became cooler. The natural air-conditioning of Mahagiri was kicking in. Home was not far away now.

Halfway up the mountain, we passed a row of small shacks, and the train crawled down to a snail's pace until it stopped. Sud-denly, the train's compartment was filled with vendors, mostly small boys, carrying a variety of things to sell. I made the mistake of smiling at a boy carrying a stack of potato *bondas*. He twisted a piece of newspaper into a cone, and, using a thin napkin, he dropped some snacks into the paper cup. "Take it, *Akka*," he said, using the local word for older sister.

I wanted to refuse. I knew how unhealthy deep-fried foods were, and my mother had never encouraged us to eat street food. She hated the thought of the flies sitting on the open carts.

But my mother wasn't here and I didn't see any flies so I accepted the paper cone. It was warm to my touch.

"How much?" I asked him.

"My friend has hot tea," he said, gesturing with his head.

Another youngster appeared at his shoulder. He was bone-thin and carrying a metal wire tray with small glasses of tea. I sighed, in for a *bonda* and all the other stuff.

"Alright, I'll take tea. And I'm giving you a few extra rupees for a *bonda* and tea. Promise me, you'll use the money for food."

In unison, the boys glanced at each other and said, "Yes, *Akka*, yes."

I took out my purse and pulled out my wallet. I handed a few rupee notes to the *bonda* seller and then held out a steel cup.

"Pour the tea in this," I told the tea boy.

"You travel with your own cup, *Akka*?"

He sounded so amazed I had to laugh out loud.

"My mother always said I should use my cup when traveling."

He carefully poured the tea into my cup and handed it to me, "*Akka*, you are lucky to have such a caring mother."

His voice was wistful, and I nodded before replying, "Yes, I am, but she would not approve of roadside snacks."

"Well, these are train side snacks," the *bonda* seller said with a mischievous grin.

With one final smile, the boys went in search of new customers. I took a sip of warm tea. It was strong and sweet, and I smiled at the familiar taste. The *bondas* were filled with spicy potatoes, sharp with green chilies, and tangy with lemon juice. They tasted wonderful with the sweet tea, and I enjoyed them without feeling guilty. I licked the last bit of the chickpea flour coating off my fingers and sighed happily. Now, it felt like I was indeed coming home.

CHAPTER TWO
HOME AT LAST

The match-stick train finally pulled into the small, charming station in Mahagiri. The station was a one-of-a-kind place, famous because it had been featured in many Tamil movies where star-crossed lovers sang sad goodbyes before boarding the train. It had even been the set for a couple of British period-piece dramas. I had a lot of luggage and looked out the window for a porter. I spotted a familiar face.

"Sam," I called out.

Sam, or Sampath, was a young man who worked as a porter at the train and bus stations. He had been helping me in and out of trains and buses since I went to college. I've known him for a long time. He was now married with a young child.

"Missy," he called back with a huge grin. "Welcome home. I don't see your driver."

"No one knows I'm coming home," I said. "It's a surprise. Can you help me with my bags and call a taxi?"

A few minutes later, I was settled in a taxi. I waved to Sam and directed the driver to take me to my mother's house.

When the car pulled to the gate, I saw that the tall jacaranda tree was still guarding the front yard. The driver was about to honk his car horn.

"Don't honk," I said. "Just drop my things at the gate."

He turned around with a look of surprise and asked, "Are you sure, miss? I can easily drive you to the front porch."

"No," I said. "I want to surprise my family."

I got out my wallet and handed him some rupee notes. He took them before getting out and pulling my bags out of the trunk. He piled them beside the tall tree and drove off, muttering something about crazy young women.

I stood for a moment, looking around. Everything was familiar and dear, but I felt like a stranger. Coming home is a lot harder than it seems. I pushed open the gate, which creaked as loudly as I remembered. A little girl ran down the driveway to see who had opened the gate.

"Bindita, is that you?" I called out to my niece. She stopped abruptly and stared at me. "It's your aunty Sunny."

She grinned and ran back to the house. I could hear her calling for her mother and her granny.

"What is it, Bindita?" I heard my sister Meena's voice before I saw her coming out of the house. My niece held her hand and pulled her toward the front gate, where I stood awkwardly holding a large suitcase.

Meena stopped for a second and stared at me.

"Sunny? Gosh, what are you doing here?" she asked as she approached me. "Why didn't you tell us you were coming?"

She didn't wait for me to answer but pushed the gate open before rushing through it. She pulled me into her arms, a familiar place for me, and I hugged her back, taking a deep breath of that unique scent of Meena. She smelled of boiled tea, French perfume, and home cooking. She drew away and looked at me with affection. I was touched to see tears in her eyes.

"Little Sunny, I missed you!" she said. "I can't believe you are here. I know you were finishing your internship, but we weren't expecting you until next month."

I gazed into her warm brown eyes. She was as gorgeous as ever.

"I missed you too, *chechi*," I said. "I mean Meena."

A few years ago, she had admonished me for calling her *chechi* or big sister and had insisted I call her Meena.

She laughed, and we both turned to see my mother coming down the driveway.

"Thangam? Is everything alright?"

"Yes, Amma," I said.

"Then why are you standing like a mendicant at the gate? Come in. You don't need an invitation."

My mother always called me Thangam. I could never get her to call me Sunny.

"Oh, Amma," I said, tearful and emotional, "I know, but I just wanted to stand here a moment and enjoy this place."

"Well, you can finish enjoying it inside," she said firmly. She took my hand in her careworn one and peered up at me.

"Hmm, you look tired and thin. It's good you're home. Let's get you to the kitchen. We can find something for you to eat and drink."

Since it was early spring, the front yard still had a desolate air about it. The blooms and blossoms were still just buds, waiting to open. I felt a fleeting sympathy for them. I thought I, too, was just waiting to bloom.

My old babysitter, Kashi, rushed to help me with my bags.

My niece led us through the front parlor and dining room into the kitchen, the heart and soul of our home.

"Where are your children?" I asked Kashi. When Kashi was a teenager, she was our babysitter, and we all loved her. She married Raman, another cowhand, and had two young children.

"With Raman's mother," she replied. "I'll bring them by later so you can meet them."

Before I could reply, I was engulfed in another hug. I pulled back to grin at Devi, who was hugging me tightly. Her embrace smelled like raw onions, and I smiled into her shoulder.

She had been peeling pearl onions, and I could see them on the kitchen table looking like a pile of glistening purple gems.

"*Kutty*, how did you get here?" she asked.

"Devi, I came by taxi; you have heard of those, haven't you?"

She ignored my teasing.

"Taxi? Why didn't Jaibal meet you?"

Jaibal was our chauffeur and had been part of our family for a long time.

Something in my expression caused my mother to hastily interrupt.

"Devi, never mind how she got here. We are happy she is home at last. Can you make her some tea and something to eat?"

I was pushed down onto the wooden bench with Bindita by my side. I smoothed her hair. She was as beautiful as her mother.

"You are getting so big, Bindita," I said. "How old are you now?"

"Aunty, I'm eight, and I'm going to be a *chechi*," she said.

I looked over at Meena, who was blushing. She nodded at me and said, "In seven long months."

I smiled. "I can't wait. I hope to be here when you give birth."

"Are you planning on staying, then?"

"I'm not sure yet."

I was glad when Kashi came in and interrupted us.

"Bindita, let's go and take your bath, and afterward, your aunty can come to say your evening prayers with you."

"Will you, Aunty?"

"Of course," I said, sipping the tea. Devi had put a plate of chips and nuts before me, but I had no appetite. I took another sip of hot tea and put down the cup.

"Bring Bandita to the memorial," Meena told Kashi. "Sunny, have you had enough tea?"

I nodded and said, "*Amma*, let's walk out to the backyard."

The three of us walked through the open courtyard to the back of the house. Parts of the garden were tilled and ready for planting. Soon, the garden would be filled with all kinds of growing things. Meena and my mother led me to the far end of the backyard, where a cement wall had been built. The partially enclosed space had several flower pots adding a splash of color with a pedestal in the center containing the sacred *tulsi* plant in an earthen pot. The wall was about three feet tall, made of solid grey cement, and about five feet long. On top of the wall were bunches of cut flowers, some turning old and crisp. Several metal plaques were mounted on the wall, each one polished to a bright sheen. The largest one in the center was inscribed: *Death is not extinguishing the light; it is only putting out the lamp because the dawn has come~~Rabindranath Tagore.*

Just below this quote was an alcove that contained a small oil lamp, an incense stick holder, and a pack of matches.

The wall had several other metal plaques dedicated to different family members. I ran my fingers over the one for my father. *Acha.*

One was for Mac, Muthi, and even our old nanny, Ayah.

The sun was setting, and it was getting cool. I had missed these magical Mahagiri sunsets where the world turned pink and gold.

"I come here every evening to talk to your father and pay my respects to the others," my mother said.

She sat down on the long stone bench, and Meena and I sat down on either side of her. The space was colorful, with many pots of blooming flowers. There were flowering bushes along the wall, and the air was fragrant.

"It's beautiful, Ma, and so peaceful," I sighed deeply.

I placed my head on my mother's shoulder and said, "I miss all of them, especially *Achan.*"

My mother patted my knee before replying, "I know, Thangam, I know. Sometimes it seems like life should stop when you lose a loved one, but the world keeps turning, and life goes on."

She turned to face me, and I lifted my head to look into her eyes.

"We are so glad you are here, *kutty*," she said. "It has been a long time since we all have been together."

"I know, *Amma.* It's good to be home again."

Meena peered around my mother and said, "You look rundown and weary, Sunny. You must rest and get fat on Devi's and Amma's cooking."

I laughed and said, "I would like that and then figure out where I'm going to practice."

"What? Aren't you going to practice at the local hospital?" Meena asked.

Before I could reply, my mother said, "Meena, let the girl rest, and we can talk later."

The three of us sat in front of the stone memorial in companionable silence. I knew this silence and peace wouldn't last forever.

CHAPTER THREE

BHOJAN'S IDEA

True to her word, my mother, Meena, and Devi prepared a delicious evening meal featuring my favorite foods. Meena had also learned some new dishes during her stay in California. I loved the stir-fried veggies, pungent with garlic and ginger and tangy with fresh lime juice.

The following day, after the bustle of milking the cows and getting Bindita off to school, I went on a solitary walk. The air was clear and crisp. The sun was warm on my bare head as I wandered through the pear orchard and the tea plantation. In the distance, I could see a worker repairing the fence. I walked over and was delighted to find Bhojan.

I have known Bhojan all my life. He was one of the original cow hands my mother hired when she first started her milking business as a newly married young woman. His daughter, Kashi, was now helping Devi in the kitchen.

"Bhojan," I called out.

Bhojan turned around and wiped his forehead with the back of his hand.

"*Kutty*," he said. "I heard you came home last night by taxi. It's good to see you; we have missed you."

I smiled. I was forever a "kutty or child" when I came home.

"Bhojan, it is Dr. Sunny now," I said teasingly.

Bhojan laughed and stood up slowly, his hand on his back.

"Ahh," he said. "I'll remember to call you Dr. Sunny. Can you handle all my aches and pains, Dr. Sunny?"

I walked over to him and touched his shoulder.

"Are you in pain?"

He shook his head and replied, "No, no, *kutty*. I mean, doctor, just old age."

"I can take a look at you when we get back," I said. "There is medicine now that will help with some of the aches of old age."

Bhojan motioned with his hand to follow him, and we walked up the slope together. He stopped at a large flat rock and sat down. I joined him.

Mahagiri Valley was spread out in front of us. The distant hills were a hazy blue-green, and a deep canyon was below us. I could see the city of Pellaur beyond the valley. The view had an end-of-the-world feeling to it. The sun was warm on my face, and I stretched out my legs with a slight sigh.

"Here." Bhojan was holding out a handful of red fruit. "You girls always loved these guavas."

The tiny red guavas were a childhood favorite with their tart flavor. The tree was very tall and spindly, and as children, we used to persuade Bhojan or Raman to pick some of the fruit.

"I haven't had these in years," I said, taking the fruit and popping one into my mouth.

The unique flavor of the tiny guava burst onto my tongue, filling my mouth with sweet piquancy.

I looked up to see Bhojan watching me.

"What's the matter, Bhojan?"

He didn't say anything for a long moment.

"I was thinking, Dr. Sunny, that you look too thin and lost."

Bhojan was uneducated, but he was a perceptive old man. His wise old eyes saw too much, and now he was trying to look right into my soul.

"I'm thin because I've been working hard," I said. "I'm not lost; I'm home now and happy I'm done with medical school."

"Alright, if you aren't lost, why do your eyes look so sad?"

I didn't reply right away. I licked my lips; they tasted of guava.

"I'm not lost or sad, just feeling a little out of sorts. I've been offered a position in Madras at a good private hospital."

"So, you are leaving again?"

"That's just it, Bhojan; I don't want to go. I want to stay here."

I tried to explain my mixed feelings to Bhojan.

"I was tempted to stay away, but then I realized just like Meena did, I love this place. I have Mahagiri in my blood; no other place feels like home. The whole time I was away, I couldn't wait to return. I wanted to be with Amma, Meena, you, and even the cows. At the same time, coming home means I'm a *kutty* again. I don't want to lose myself and become the second daughter."

"I can understand, Dr. Sunny," Bhojan said slowly and thoughtfully. "You will always be a *kutty* here, but you are now a grown woman, a qualified doctor who needs to find a place for herself."

"I know, Bhojan," I said with a sigh. "It's harder than you think."

"You are thinking too hard," he replied. He stood up. "I have an idea."

"What?"

He shook his head before replying, "I'll have to show you. Tomorrow, come with us when we deliver milk."

He sounded mysterious and refused to say anything more. He added, "You must wait until tomorrow, Sunny."

CHAPTER FOUR
A NEW VILLAGE

"Long ago, Mahagiri was one kingdom ruled by native King Kalaraj. The neighboring king from the Hoysala kingdom decided he wanted all the native people to obey him. He had a large army and threatened to invade Mahagiri. Kalaraj was a brave man, and he fought the Hoysala army and was killed. Even though he lost the war and his kingdom, the people loved his bravery and heroism. Our village is named Kalarajanad after the brave king." As told by Ari.

The following day, I woke up early and dressed in warm clothes and walking shoes before going to the kitchen. As usual, it was a busy place. I missed Muthi at the coffee table, dispensing everyone's morning drink. Kashi had taken over and smiled at me as she handed me a hot drink. I wrapped my fingers around the steel tumbler and walked into the cooking area where Devi was preparing breakfast. The room was warm and smelled of rice and coconut. I peered over her shoulder.

"What are you making, Devi?"

She turned around and smiled at me. "*Kutty*, I'm making *puttu* and chickpea curry. Why are you up so early?"

I sipped my coffee and watched her fill the cylindrical *puttu* canister with ground-up rice and fresh coconut. The *puttu* was steamed in a unique mold and served with a very spicy chick-pea curry.

"I'm going with Bhojan on his milk rounds this morning," I said.

"Are you going to become a milk doctor?"

I smiled. "Maybe. Bhojan said he wanted to show me something. What time does he leave?"

"Soon, they are just finishing loading the milk cans, but you have time for a *puttu* and curry."

I was just finishing the last bite when Bhojan walked in.

"Dr. Sunny, are you ready?"

"Let me get a coat, and I'll join you."

"We are by the cowshed," he said. "Raman is driving the big jeep."

I quickly brushed my teeth, combed my hair, and picked up a coat and scarf. I paused in front of the mirror and stared at my reflection. I *was* too skinny. I had lost a lot of weight. I tucked a curl behind my ear. My hair was long and curly like Meena's, and we both had large almond-shaped eyes, our father's eyes. My nose was tiny, and the skin stretched tight across my cheekbones, giving me a gaunt look. Yes, I needed to put on some weight and look healthier. A weak and sick doctor wasn't going to inspire confidence. *Physician heal thyself.*

Meena, my mother, and Bindita were in the dining room.

"Where are you off to?" Meena asked. "We're just about to go drop Bindita at school. Want to come with us?"

"Aunty, come with us," Bindita said, jumping up and down.

"I can't come with you today, Bindita," I said. "I'm going with Bhojan and Raman."

"Delivering milk?" my mother asked with a frown.

"Yes," I replied, not elaborating.

My mother raised her eyebrows but didn't ask any more questions.

"Well, we'll see you when you get back."

I hugged Bindita and promised to take her to school tomorrow.

I could hear Meena asking my mother what that was all about as I walked out the front door. I didn't wait to hear my mother's reply.

Bhojan and Raman were already seated in the jeep. The back of the vehicle was filled with metal milk cans. I climbed into the back seat. I was glad I had my scarf and coat because it was cold in the open-air jeep. We made numerous stops, and Raman jumped out from the driver's seat each time to unload a milk can. When he was delivering milk to a local preschool, I leaned over. I asked Bhojan, "Delivering milk with you and Raman brings back many memories, but what did you want to show me?"

Bhojan turned to look at me and said, "Dr. Sunny, we are going to the small village of Kalarajanad, which is not too far from Lower Mahagiri. I thought I'd introduce you to a relative who lives in the village."

I sat back and thought about what he had just said.

He added, "Dr. Sunny, it's a short visit to see this village, nothing more."

"Alright," I said, taking a deep breath. "I don't understand what the secrecy is about."

Bhojan chuckled and said, "I thought you might find this village interesting."

I was about to ask another question, but Bhojan raised his hand and said, "Just wait until we get there."

When Raman was done delivering milk, he turned the jeep around and drove toward Kalarajanad.

We passed Lower Mahagiri, the fruit market, and the large government hospital. We turned off the main thoroughfare onto a much narrower road. It was paved, but large potholes made it a rough ride. After several kilometers, Raman turned onto an even narrower road. The drive got really rough now. The jeep bounced along, and I held onto the seat, fearing being tossed out of the vehicle. The hills on either side of us were covered with tea bushes. It was also quite foggy now, and the thick grey mist was so dense that it clung to my hair and eyelashes in fat droplets. The jeep had an overhead canopy and offered no real protection from the cold and damp. The vehicle crested over a hill, and we drove to a small valley. I leaned out the window and saw a cluster of buildings in the distance. Raman drove a few more feet and stopped before a huge tree. I pushed open the jeep door and climbed out.

The air was heavy with moisture, but the sun was starting to pierce through the thick fog here in the clearing, and I could feel its meager warmth on my face. The hillsides were carpeted in Mahagiri's 'green gold.' The tea bushes were planted in rows, with spindly trees growing between them. I knew these were the quinine-producing trees. Medicinal quinine was necessary in treating malaria. Bhojan and Raman were already walking toward the houses, and I hurried to catch up. Around the tree's base, the villagers had built a short brick wall, and I saw a couple of men seated cross-legged on it. They had been talking but fell silent as we approached. One called out, "Strangers, can I help you?"

Bhojan approached the elderly man wearing a white dhoti and a long blue woolen coat. He had a thick turban on his head and a pair of brown spectacles perched at the tip of his large nose. He pushed his glasses up and looked at us with interest.

"Big father," Bhojan addressed him in respectful tones. "We are from Mahagiri…"

"This, too, is part of Mahagiri," the man said.

"Of course, I meant we are from the town."

"I know what you meant. Continue.," he said in a gruff tone.

"My cousin Ranga lives here," Bhojan started to say but was interrupted by the older man.

"Ranga is your cousin, why didn't you say so? Come, you must visit my house."

He turned to his friend and said, "I'll be back. These visitors are relatives of a relative.

"My name is Ari, and I'm the headman of this village," he continued. "You must meet my wife, who is Ranga's cousin, and so, in a way, we are related."

"I'm Bhojan," Bhojan said as he introduced himself. "This is..."

The man stopped him with a hand gesture and replied, "There will be plenty of time to talk."

He continued walking quickly down the path.

"This temple is dedicated to Lord Ganesha," our guide pointed to a small shrine. "We are an unusual village in that it comprises several different communities. We have several Brahmin families, one of which cares for this temple. Some tradesmen live here and work in Lower Mahagiri. We also have some people from as far away as Mysore and Kerala."

"How did the village get its name?" I asked.

Ari looked surprised when I spoke. Perhaps he hadn't realized I could talk.

"The village is named after a well-known and brave King. His name was Kalaraja. We are a diverse community of people, all living together," he answered. "The Carmelite nuns found out about this place and opened a nunnery, so Christians live here as well."

"And does everyone live in harmony?" I asked.

"Well, it is like any other village; we have our disputes, but they are not usually based on religion," he said. "Ahh, this is my house. Come in, come in."

He led us to a large, well-portioned house on the outskirts of the small village. A small vegetable garden was in front, surrounded by a wire fence. He opened the flimsy gate, and we followed him down a dirt-packed path. Rose bushes and some other plants were on either side of the path. The house had a small veranda where we stopped to remove our shoes before entering the main living room. It was a long, spacious room with wooden chairs and a long bench. There was a narrow wooden table against one corner. Ari indicated we sit down and walked inside through one of the three doorways.

He came back a few minutes later and sat facing us in one of the chairs.

"My wife Nandi will bring us some tea. Now, tell me who you are and why you are here."

Bhojan spoke for all of us. "As I mentioned, my name is Bhojan, and you may have heard of the Big House and Little Mother."

"Yes, of course, I have heard of that good lady."

"Well, this is Dr. Sunny. She is the youngest daughter of Little Mother and has recently graduated from medical school."

"Ahh," Ari said, looking at me with a speculative look. "I see, and what are you all doing here?"

Bhojan unwound his turban to scratch his head before replying, "I had heard from my cousin Ranga that there is no doctor in this village."

Ari was about to speak up, but I glared at Bhojan. "Bhojan, can I talk to you for a moment? Outside?"

I turned to Ari. "Please excuse us, but I need to ask Bhojan a question in private."

The headman nodded, looking confused. I couldn't blame him because I felt the same way as I walked to the veranda. I wrapped my arms around me and waited for Bhojan to join me. Raman was talking to a group of men and watched us with curious eyes. He was probably wondering if we were ready to drive back home.

As soon as Bhojan stepped outside, I turned to him and asked, "Bhojan, why did you bring me here?"

He held up a hand to stop my angry torrent of words, "*Kutty*, I mean, Dr. Sunny, I just wanted you to see this place and perhaps consider opening a practice here."

"In this village?" I asked.

"Yes, you mentioned you wanted to live in Mahagiri but not in your mother's or big sister's shadow. This seemed like a perfect compromise. An ideal place to establish your practice and independence."

As I listened to him, I could understand the wisdom and thought behind his actions.

"It sounds good in theory, Bhojan," I said. "However, I don't like being surprised."

"I'm sorry, Dr. Sunny. I just thought this might be a good option."

I gnawed on my lower lip. "I don't know...."

"You don't have to decide anything right now. Let's go back inside and talk to Ari," Bhojan said, taking my elbow. I let him lead me back inside, even though I wasn't sure about the situation.

Ari stood up when we entered the room and indicated we sit down.

He asked, "Is everything alright?"

I nodded, and Bhojan said, "As I was saying, my cousin says you don't have a village doctor?"

Ari nodded slowly before replying, "Yes, that is true. For the past two years, our families have traveled to Lower Mahagiri when we needed to see a doctor. Besides, the people in Kalarajanad, there are many small villages within walking distance that also need a doctor."

Bhojan asked, "Are you looking for a doctor? Do you have any applicants?"

Ari was taken aback at the question. "We aren't exactly looking, but..."

Just then, Nandi came in bearing a tea tray. She was dressed in traditional Bhadaga robes and had a large gold ring on her nose. She smiled shyly at me as she placed the tray on the table. She handed each of us a steel cup of hot tea. She looked at me and asked, "You are a qualified doctor?"

"Yes, I am," I said, putting the teacup down.

Nandi said, "I was wondering if I could speak to you privately."

Ari frowned. "I don't think that is a good idea, Nandi."

I looked at Nandi and replied. "I can speak with you, Nandi, but I can't treat you as my patient."

"See," Ari said. "That is what I was trying to say."

"Then, call it a private meeting," Nandi said. "Please come with me, doctor."

Ari started to say something else but stopped himself. I followed Nandi through the doorway into another larger room. She led me to a sofa and indicated I sit down. There was a radio and television on one side of the room and several oversized chairs. It seemed like a comfortable room. I couldn't believe I was in a remote village.

"Doctor," she began to say. "I don't know how to ask this..."

"My name is Sunny," I said.

She smiled at me. "That is a happy name."

I had to smile back. "Now tell me, what's wrong? Are you in pain?"

"Yes," she said, looking down at her hands. "I'm not comfortable talking about my problems."

"I understand. Just tell me, is it something a woman experiences?"

She looked at me and said, "Yes, I'm not sure how to say this, but I have a terrible itch down there." She was indicating her groin area.

I nodded. "I can't prescribe any medicine until I've examined you, and I'm not approved to practice here."

She looked so crestfallen that I wanted to help her. I thought for a moment. I remembered how Ayah treated women in our household for similar complaints.

"I can't prescribe any medicine. But there are some simple home methods to temporarily relieve the itching. Do you have garlic?"

"Yes, of course. We grow our own."

"Then make tea by boiling some garlic and drink as much as possible. Also, dry the area well after bathing and apply some warm coconut oil. These are temporary solutions. You will still need to go to the hospital and be examined."

"Oh, thank you, Dr. Sunny; you are like your name, full of sunshine and good fortune," Nandi said with tears in her eyes.

I smiled and then had an idea and asked, "Nandi, why don't you come with us today? We can go to the government hospital. Is there a bus you can take to come back home?"

"Oh, yes, Dr. Sunny," she said excitedly. "One bus goes through the village in the morning and returns at night. So, I can take the bus back from Lower Mahagiri."

Nandi was so relieved that she nearly ran to the living room.

"The doctor has agreed to help me," she said to her husband, who looked slightly bewildered. "She's going to take me to the hospital, and I can return on the night bus."

Ari stood up. He looked alarmed as he asked, "Is your condition so dire you need to go to the hospital right now?"

I put a reassuring hand on his arm and said, "No, no, Mr. Ari. She is just uncomfortable. If she gets the proper medicine, she will feel better."

He didn't look very reassured, but Nandi was already throwing a heavily embroidered shawl around her shoulder. She slipped her bare feet into some sturdy plastic sandals and looked at me.

"Well, Dr. Sunny, I'm ready."

"Perhaps I should come along," Ari said. "We can go to Woodlands Hotel for dinner afterward."

Nandi grinned at her husband, and soon we were climbing into our jeep on the way to Lower Mahagiri. Perhaps it was the company or my brain playing tricks on me, but the trip down to Mahagiri seemed much quicker. Raman pulled the jeep into the government hospital parking lot.

"Why don't you and Bhojan get some tea and a snack while I get Nandi checked in?" I suggested to the men.

I asked the guard at the front gate for directions to the hospital director's office. I turned to Nandi and Ari.

"Why don't you wait here," I said, pointing to the waiting room. "I'll talk to the director and then come get you."

I left the couple and wandered down the hallway until I found the one belonging to the hospital director. He was in his office and quickly got up to greet me.

He was an older man with graying hair and a gentle demeanor, and I immediately liked him.

"Namaskar," I said as I introduced myself.

"My good name is Balakrishnan," he replied. "Please sit down, Dr. Sunny."

I explained Nandi's condition and how I came to meet her.

"I think she has a urinary tract infection. I persuaded her to come here to get tested and get some antibiotics if that is the correct diagnosis."

He nodded and said, "Of course. I will see that Nandi is taken care of. But tell me why you were visiting the village?"

"Dr. Balakrishnan, I just completed my general practitioner training," I replied. "And have been offered a job in Madras. My family has lived in Mahagiri for many years, and I'm home for a visit. A friend of the family has relatives in Kalarajanad."

"You say you have family here? Would I know them?"

I smiled and replied, "You probably have heard of my mother. Everyone calls her Little Mother."

"Of course, you are Sudha's daughter. I knew one of her children was going to medical school. I just didn't put two and two together. Old age," he said with a deprecating laugh.

He stood up when he saw a nurse through the open doorway.

He called out her name, "Nurse Anna."

She came into the office, and I stood up.

"This is Dr. Sunny, Sudha's little girl. She's brought us a patient."

The head nurse stared at me.

"You are not going to believe this, Dr. Sunny, but I was one of the nurses at the hospital the day you and your brother were born. I feel as if I know you already."

I laughed. This is what happens when you come home.

"So, who is the patient?" Anna asked, now speaking in a professional manner.

"Her name is Nandi, and she is in the waiting room by the front door," I said. "I think she might have a UTI."

The nurse nodded. "I'll show her to exam room 4 if you want to stop by."

"Thank you," I said.

The nurse turned to face me, asking, "So, will you join our staff?"

I shrugged. "I haven't decided on anything yet. I'm still recovering from medical school."

"I understand," she said with a smile. "We would welcome you here. Not many young people return to their hometown after finishing university."

I took leave of Dr. Balakrishan.

"Thank you again for your help," I said.

He shook my hand and said, "It's not my place to give you counsel, but that village and surrounding area could use a young, enthusiastic doctor. I'm sure the hospital board would be eager to hire you. The hospital will pay your salary and provide housing. You would have hospital privileges and the help of all our professional staff."

He did make it sound enticing and I thanked him and added, "I have never considered being a village doctor, but my trip today was educational and an eye-opener."

I waited outside exam room 4, and soon, Nandi came out with a piece of paper.

"Dr. Sunny, they gave me a prescription for some medicine. My husband and I will pick it up before going to Hotel Woodlands. Will you join us?"

Before I could reply, Nandi turned to Nurse Anna and said, "We are hoping to convince Dr. Sunny to become our village doctor."

"She would make a great village doctor," Anna said. "I hope to see you soon, Dr. Sunny."

I tried to tamper Nandi's enthusiasm. "Nandi, I was just helping you today. I'm not sure I would even make a good village doctor."

"Can't you see how you helped me? Many women and children in the village need a doctor."

"This is all happening too fast," I said.

"Just come and visit us again," she said. "I will clean the clinic; the doctor's residence is next door."

"I will think about it," I said, unsure what I agreed to. "Come on, let's find your husband."

We walked out to the waiting room, where Ari was pacing.

"Ah, there you are," he said to his wife. "Is everything alright?"

"It's all fine," she said. "We will need to pick up some medicine. I was trying to convince Dr. Sunny to be our village doctor."

Ari looked surprised.

"A woman doctor. I'm not sure that would work," he said.

"We need a doctor, and what is wrong with a woman doctor?" Nandi asked. "She is qualified, and she helped me today. The village has no doctor, husband."

Her voice was stern but respectful. She turned to me.

"Come for a visit with your mother," she told me. "I'll give you a tour of the clinic and the doctor's house."

I replied, "Let me talk to my mother, and then we'll see."

I left the couple and found Raman and Bhojan waiting for me.

While Raman turned the jeep around, Bhojan asked me, "So, is Nandi alright?"

"She will be fine," I said.

I paused and said, "She's pushing me to be the village doctor."

"Yes, she is the real boss," Raman laughed.

Bhojan was silent. I turned to him and asked, "Why are you so quiet? Wasn't this what you had in mind?"

He smiled at me and said, "You know, *kutty*, Dr. Sunny, sometimes you sound just like your mother. I was thinking of old Ayah, who used to write down her herbal remedies for potions and oils in a notebook. I think your mother might still have it."

"I'll ask her," I said. "And Bhojan, this was a good idea. It has given me a lot to think about. I need to talk to Amma."

I couldn't wait to get home and tell my mother about my day.

CHAPTER FIVE
PREPARATIONS

We reached home past lunchtime, but I was too excited to feel hungry.

"Come on, Sunny, you have to eat something," Devi said as she handed me one of her famous roti rolls.

This was a family favorite when we traveled by train. Potatoes flavored with ginger and fresh lemon juice were rolled inside fresh whole wheat rotis (chapattis). It was the perfect travel and finger food.

I took one from the plate and nibbled on it. I was too busy to eat because I was telling my mother about my morning adventures.

"You did all that in one morning?" my mother asked. She sounded amazed. "What an enterprising young woman you are."

I blushed. "Amma, you know Bhojan took me to the village because he thought I might be interested in working as a village doctor."

My mother didn't say anything.

I crumbled the last bit of roti with my fingers, looked down at my plate, and said, "I think Bhojan may be on to something."

My mother looked astonished.

"But you always said you couldn't wait to leave and get a job in a big city."

"I know," I said with a sad nod. "I thought that is what I wanted until I started to miss Mahagiri."

"Now, you want to live in Mahagiri?"

I nodded and looked up.

"This morning, it was so rewarding to help Nandi with her problem. She was so grateful. I'm not sure I'll have that personal connection in a big city hospital."

My mother stared at me. "So, you want to be a village doctor?"

I hesitated before replying, "I wasn't sure I wanted to move back here. I love you, Meena, and everyone else, but I'm just *kutty* again when I'm here."

My mother sighed and said, "Oh, Thangam. You will always be my *kutty*, but we are aware you are now a grown woman and a qualified doctor."

Now, it was my turn to stare at her.

I shrugged my shoulder. "You understand?"

"Of course, I do," my mother said, smiling at me. "You didn't want to live in our shadow, and I know how hard it must have been for you growing up as the younger daughter. Perhaps being a village doctor will allow you to find your own wings."

I didn't know what to say. My mother was always surprising me.

She added. "Perhaps you can show me this village?"

I sat up and asked, "Do you mean that?"

"Yes, let's visit and have a look around, and then you can make up your mind," my mother replied. "If that is what you want, of course."

I've always known my mother supported us in all the important ways. She had wanted to arrange Meena's marriage. Still, she finally agreed that teaching her self-sufficiency was more important than marriage. Meena had met Raj on a plane, and eventually, things had worked out, and now they were married. It was reassuring to know she wanted me to find my way in the world, too.

CHAPTER SIX
ANOTHER TRIP

The following week, I once again climbed into the jeep. Jaibal was driving us today. Bhojan and I sat in the back seat while my mother sat up front with Jaibal.

The morning fog was already lifting, and the green hills gleamed in the warm sunshine. We had been driving for about an hour when my mother spoke up.

"This is a beautiful part of Mahagiri. I don't think I've ever visited this particular village."

We drove up the hill and then onto the large meadow. Nandi was waiting for us under the large tree. She waved and came up to the car.

"Dr. Sunny," she said, "I'm so happy to see you."

She turned to my mother.

"This is my mother," I said, but Nandi waved aside my introduction.

"We have heard of Little Mother. She is well-known in Mahagiri," Nandi said. "Little Mother, welcome to Kalarajanad. We are honored to have you here."

We walked down the path to Nandi's house, where she had tea waiting for us.

"Have some tea," Nandi said, putting a steel tumbler before my mother. "Did your daughter tell you how she helped me?"

My mother smiled at the woman and sipped hot tea before replying, "Yes, she was glad to help you."

Nandi looked at us and said, "We need a good doctor in this village. I hope I can convince your daughter to be that doctor."

My mother said nothing, so I spoke up. "Nandi, are you feeling better?"

"I'm much better," she replied. She wagged a finger at me, "You are clever to change the subject, but I'm not done convincing you."

I laughed and took a sip of tea. Nandi started to pour us more tea, but I declined.

"Well, if you have finished your tea, would you like a clinic tour?"

Nandi looked so anxious. I felt sorry for her, but my mother now spoke up, "Of course. Thank you for the tea, Nandi."

"The clinic is just a short walk from here," Nandi said, pointing to a building a few yards down the hill.

As we walked down the path, my mother asked, "What happened to your previous doctor?"

Nandi stopped in mid-stride and shook her head.

"It is a sad story," she said. "He was a good man and doctor. We all loved him, but as he got older, he became forgetful. One night, the doctor went on a house call without his driver, and we found him wandering by the river, far from his jeep in the morning. That's when we realized he needed care. He went to live with relatives back in his native village. It was a sad day for us. That was over two years ago, and we have been waiting for a replacement doctor ever since."

We all resumed walking and soon arrived at a long, squat brick building. We went up the porch steps and onto the veranda.

"This space could use some plants," my mother said, looking around. "Or even a small garden."

"The clinic is through this door," Nandi said, pushing the heavy wooden door open.

We stepped into a large waiting room that smelled of cleaning supplies. There was a long wooden table, a bench, and several chairs.

"A group of us cleaned and scrubbed this place," Nandi said. "This is the waiting room, and that door leads to the exam room, and this one leads to the doctor's living quarters."

She pointed to the doors on either side of the waiting room. I walked across the bare wooden floorboards, which were well-worn. The walls could have used a fresh coat of paint, but everything was clean and dust-free.

"You've done a great job," I said to Nandi, who blushed as she pushed open a door.

I sighed at seeing the exam room with its large bed for examining patients. It was a simple setup with just a few chairs, a small wooden desk, and a wash basin with a tap. I strangely felt at home. I tapped my mother's arm.

"Amma," I said. "This place has so much potential."

She looked at me with bright eyes and said, "Maybe you have found your place."

Nandi had been watching us and now spoke up.

"This metal filing cabinet, as well as a locked wooden cupboard, is for patient records and medicine."

I looked around and imagined my degrees framed and hanging on the walls. Perhaps some color prints of the green hills on another wall? An anatomy chart on another?

Nandi and my mother had moved on to the doctor's living space, but I wanted to relish a few more moments in this room. I closed my eyes and tried to picture myself wearing a white lab coat and talking to patients. I opened my eyes. Maybe this was the place to start my career.

I followed the voices of my mother and Nandi to a long living room. There was a small wooden table and a single chair, but it looked like it needed to be cozier and more welcoming.

I peeked into the bedroom, which contained a bed. There was a brand-new mattress on the ground, waiting to be put on the bed . There was a large window with a breathtaking view of the valley. The morning sun was cresting over the hills, and the valley was bathed in yellow sunshine. In the distance, I could make out a cluster of houses and a sizeable meadow-like area beyond that. There was a bathroom adjoining the bedroom. I noted there was a tap for cold water but not for hot water.

My mother was in the kitchen with Nandi, looking through cupboards.

"I guess stocking this room won't be your priority," she said teasingly.

"Don't worry, Little Mother," Nandi said. "I'll cook all her meals and make sure she eats well."

"See," I said with a laugh, "I won't have to learn to cook after all."

My mother shook her head and said, "If you work here, making your coffee or hot drink would be nice."

"So, what do you think?" Nandi asked eagerly. "Can you see yourself working here?"

I smiled at her enthusiasm.

"It has a lot of promise," I said.

"But?" Nandi asked nervously.

"I'm not sure," I said. I looked over at my mother, who stared back at me.

"What do you think, Amma?"

My mother was silent for a long moment, and I was worried she was finding everything wrong with this place.

"I think Thangam, a village doctor, might be just the thing for you."

"Really?"

Nandi watched us with worried eyes and said, "There are several villages, some far and some close, but this is an excellent place to reach them all.

"The Carmelite mission is not too far from here, and the nuns are very helpful to the villagers."

My mother put an arm around me. "I want you to find your own place, and this village might be a good starting point. I suggest you accept the contract temporarily and see how it works out. Of course, I'll be happy to help you settle in."

I hugged her tightly. "Thank you, Amma. I'll contact Dr. Balakrishan and talk to him about the details and organization."

Nandi couldn't help joining in a group hug.

"Dr. Sunny, you won't regret it," Nandi said. "We need a doctor and you are the woman for the job."

We walked out of the kitchen and into the living room.

"Though this room is not much," I said with a grimace.

"We'll fix it up," my mother said with a smile. "Come on, let's go home and get you ready to start your career."

We took leave of Nandi, promising to return in a few days.

"Don't forget to finish your medicine," I shouted as we drove off.

CHAPTER SEVEN

TOGETHER AGAIN

A few days after we visited the village, I was seated in my mother's kitchen, finishing my second cup of coffee, when Meena and Raj walked into the room.

"Look, Raj, it's Sunny," Meena said with a smile. "The new village doctor."

Raj smiled at me. "Hi, Sunny. I can't believe we now have two doctors in the family."

He was referring to his sister Pushpa, a practicing physician in New Delhi.

"How is your sister?" I asked, following the couple into the living room, where my mother was seated at a table. "Everyone is always surprised to hear I'm related to the famous Dr. Pushpa."

"She's busy, operating on the rich and famous or volunteering at the free clinic in her spare time, helping the less fortunate."

Dr. Pushpa was a famous cardiac surgeon, well-known for her skills in the operating room.

"Well, I'm just a humble village doctor," I said with a shrug.

"Are you kidding? Sunny, you are the talk of the town," my sister said.

That evening we shared comforting bowls of kangee.

"Devi and I have made up a great kangee recipe," my mother said, handing out bowls of the soupy rice . Instead of just rice, we've added mung beans."

The k angee o f m y c hildhood w as a c omforting b owl o f cooked rice fragrant with golden ghee and salt. We usually ate this soothing soup with pieces of raw onion; the only time I could eat raw onions as a child. My mother and Devi's version was flavored with cumin, fragrant coriander leaves, and plenty of golden ghee.

We gathered to light lamps and sticks of sandal-wood incense at the memorial in our backyard that evening. The world was bathed in the setting sun's golden light as I watched my mother light the oil lamps. The pearl-gray smoke from the incense sticks rose into the evening sky. The only person missing was my twin brother, Appu.

"You started the pooja without me?" a voice asked. I turned to find Appu standing with a duffle bag on one shoulder and a large paper bag on the other.

"Uncle Appu!" Bindita screeched, flinging herself into his arms.

"Hey there, squirt, you're getting too heavy for me," Appu said as he pretended to drop Bindita, who squealed with laughter and childish terror.

"Hey, sis," he said, hugging me with one arm as Bindita hung onto his other.

"Appu, why didn't you tell us you were coming?" Meena said as she and my mother rushed to greet him.

"You just keep getting taller and thinner," Meena said, hugging Appu.

He grinned at her and said, "Can't say the same about you."

"You..." Meena said as she playfully punched his arm.

"Hey," Raj said as he greeted Appu. "How was your trip?"

Appu worked for Raj and his father, Nandan, a successful businessman.

"All good," Appu replied, "Let's talk later, Raj."

"Come on, let's do the pooja before the sun sets," my mother said.

Appu stood next to me, his shoulder touching mine. I smiled at him. It's hard to explain but having Appu beside me felt right.

My mother started reciting the timeless words, and I closed my eyes and let my thoughts wander. I thought about Muthi, whose story I had heard a hundred times. A widow with no close family, and how she had come to live with us. She was a distant cousin, but my mother had welcomed her and made her part of the family.

Then there was our childhood nanny, Ayah. I remembered she always smelled of beedi cigarettes and brown sugar. She used to massage my scalp with warm coconut oil, heated with peppercorns and rice. She let me nibble on the crunchy rice.

The soft chants of 'Om Shanti, Om Shanti' brought me out of my reverie.

Then Meena echoed what all of us were thinking by saying, "I miss Achan so much." Her voice was thick with sorrow. Raj moved closer, and Bindita struggled to get out of Appu's arms and go to her mother.

"It seems like it was just yesterday," I said. "Appu and I were so frightened. We couldn't have lived through days without you, Meena."

"Yes, Meena was a rock," my mother said.

My father had died from a heart attack nearly sixteen years ago, but we still missed him.

"His plantation is a wonderful legacy," Raj said.

Raj's father, Nandan, had bought the plantation long before Raj and Meena married. It seemed like our lives had a way of intertwining in ways we never dreamed about.

"Your father would have wanted you to enjoy life, not think sad thoughts," my mother said. "We are all here tonight, and that's something to celebrate."

CHAPTER EIGHT

A DAY WITH FAMILY

The next day, I woke up excited and looking forward to starting my new adventure. The kitchen was bustling with activity. My mother's day always began early. Devi was at the hearth and Kashi was heating milk for coffee. Raman and another cowhand were measuring milk and straining it into large metal containers. As usual there were two cats begging for milk, one had a missing ear and eye. My mother was nowhere to be seen.

"Little Mother is in the pooja room," Devi said, noticing how I was looking around the kitchen. "She'll be here in a minute."

I nodded and walked through the inner courtyard into the storage room using the back entrance. The pooja room was a small, partitioned area within the larger storage room. The air was fragrant with ripening bananas and the dusty aroma of rice and other grains. The door to the pooja area was open and I stood at the entrance watching my mother light the oil lamps and sticks of incense. She rang the small brass bell and prostrated herself in front of all the colorful deities. Her knees cracked as she stood up. When she turned around, her face lit up and she gestured for me to join her.

"Come, Thangam," she said. She rubbed a bit of cool sandal-wood paste on my forehead. "May this day be the start of a long and prosperous journey."

In the kitchen, Kashi poured us cups of hot coffee and Devi placed a plate of fried whole wheat bread and potato curry in front of us.

"*Poories* for breakfast? Devi, you shouldn't have," I said, as I filled the tiny whole wheat bread with the flavorful potato.

These deep-fried *poories* were a favorite of mine and Appu's, but we rarely had them because my mother avoided fried foods.

"It is a special occasion," Devi said with a smile. "Your brother is here and so I thought I would make something both of you like."

Once we had eaten, I went for a walk around the orchard and by the time I got back, Appu was in the dining room with Meena and Bindita.

"Aunty," Bindita greeted me with a big hug. "Guess what?"

"What?" I said, smiling at her enthusiasm.

"Uncle Appu is taking me for a hike."

"Come with us, Sunny," my brother said. "We are going up to the flat rock."

"I love that place," Meena said. "I know, let's take a picnic with us."

"And who is going to carry this picnic?" Appu asked.

"So glad you asked, dear brother," Meena said in a sweet voice, "Of course, it will be the man's job."

"Just as I thought," Appu said pretending to be annoyed.

I hugged Bindita and both of us laughed out loud in joy. It was good to be home with Meena and Appu. It was just like old times.

"Let's go talk to Devi about what to take on this picnic," I said to Bindita.

The sun was warm on our backs as we climbed up the familiar hill behind our house. Bindita was a trooper and led the way up the steep slope. I carried a blanket while Appu had the picnic basket. When we reached the top of the hill, I spread the blanket on the familiar flat rock, and looked at the marvelous view. The valley was stretched out in front of me. The distinct blue-green hills of Mahagiri were a spectacular backdrop. I felt my heart expanding with love and gratitude for this beautiful place. Bindita came over and hugged my legs.

"What are you looking at, Aunty?"

I pointed to the far horizon and said, "Look way over there past all the hills and houses, that's where I'm going to start my practice as a village doctor."

I wasn't sure I was pointing to my actual clinic, but it was close enough for a curious young child.

"Oh, that is far away," she said.

"Not really, it looks far from here."

"Can I come visit you, Aunty?'

"I'm counting on it," I said as I bent down and picked her up. "Oof, you are getting heavy."

"I'm going to be tall too," she said.

"I don't doubt it," I said, putting her down. "Let's see what Devi has packed for our lunch."

We sat on the thick blanket and watched as Meena unpacked the basket.

"So," Appu said, sitting down beside me. "Are you ready for your next big adventure?"

I turned to look at him, squinting a little in the bright sunlight.

"I'm not sure," I said. "I'm looking forward to it, but will it be an adventure?"

When we were kids, adventure used to be our code word for something we didn't always like.

"Remember the adventure of going to boarding school and how we were so scared of going away?" I asked him.

"And didn't it turn out okay?"

"I guess it did," I replied.

Meena handed us plates loaded with my mother's famous lemon rice, a sweet and spicy mix of puffed rice and nuts, a tangy salad made from fresh corn kernels and pomegranate seeds and an array of tea biscuits made by Mala.

There was tea (from a huge thermos) and I happily dunked a biscuit in the hot beverage.

"I'm so full; I can't imagine walking down the hill," I said, wiping my mouth.

"Then you don't have to," Meena's said in triumphant voice. "I thought we'd be tired and asked Raj to come pick us up here after four."

"You think of everything, don't you?" Appu said to Meena who smiled smugly back.

Appu and I made ourselves comfortable on the blanket. We lay side by side and stared up at the bright blue sky.

"This is a perfect day," he mumbled sleepily.

I agreed.

"I'm so glad Bindita talked us all into coming."

Soon I would have to think about medical charts, patients and how to arrange my clinic but for now there was only the sun's warmth, the satisfaction of a full belly and the quiet joy of family.

A few days later, I was on my way to Kalarajanad.

Raj, Bhojan, and Jaibal had loaded the jeep with boxes. A small lorry was also filled with furniture, equipment and more boxes. A portable X-ray machine, warm blankets and sheets, a raincoat, and a large bag for my medical supplies were gifts from my family and friends. My mother's special gift was a large round spice box filled with different kinds of spices. She wanted me to learn to use them, and I had promised to try and learn to cook with them. How would I fit all these items in the small bungalow?

"Looks like you crammed everything in here," I said, checking out the medical supplies.

"It wasn't easy," Bhojan said.

The trip to the clinic seemed shorter this time, and soon, we pulled into the meadow in front of Nandi's house. We parked the vehicles in front of the clinic. The men unloaded the jeep and lorry. The front room of my cottage now had a couch, a large table, four wooden chairs, and an oversized reading chair. Bhojan arranged a lamp in one corner.

With my mother's help, I unpacked most of the supplies. She helped me put away the clothes in the wooden cupboard and made the bed with clean sheets, warm blankets, and a thick quilt. On the chest of drawers, she made a simple altar with statues of dancing Shiva, Buddha, Lord Ganesha, and baby Krishna.

"You are all set now, Thangam," she said.

I hugged her and said, "Thanks, *Amma*."

We entered the front room where Bhojan, Jaibal, and Raj were sipping tea and chatting. I heard a commotion and opened the door to the clinic to find Nandi.

"Nandi," I walked over to the headman's wife. "What is going on?"

"This is Babu," Nandi introduced the young boy by her side. "He is upset."

"Please, you have to help," he said. "The demon is revisiting big sister."

"Slow down, Babu," Nandi said. She patted the boy's shoulder.

"Please, you have to come and help. The witch is beating my sister."

Nandi looked at me, "Dr. Sunny, can you please come with me?"

I nodded and said, "Yes, of course. Let me get my medical bag."

But my mother had beaten me to it and handed me the bag I had just filled with a few basic medical supplies.

Raj came out of the building and asked, "Do you need us to come?"

I shook my head and replied, "I can manage. Besides, I need to do this on my own."

My mother said, "Raj and Bhojan, why don't you take the lorry back? And I'll come home with Jaibal in the jeep."

"Where are we going, Nandi?" I asked the older woman as we rushed out of the house and turned toward the hills.

"Babu and his family live down that valley," she said, pointing to a steep path leading down to a cluster of houses. "They sell milk from a buffalo they own, and the mother takes in washing to make some money."

"Who is the witch?" my mother asked.

I had almost forgotten she was with us. She had convinced me to let her come along to comfort the boy. She was walking behind us, holding onto Babu's hand.

"She is not really a witch…." Nandi said.

"Yes, she is," Babu said. "She can turn you into a frog if she wants."

"Oh, child," Nandi said, shaking her head. "The witch is actually a woman called Bhadra. She lives by herself in the hills and makes a living as a healer. People go to her for ailments, and she gives out potions and herbs."

We had reached the cluster of houses, and even from a distance, we could hear the screams and yelling.

"Amma, you stay here with Babu," I said, following Nandi into the house.

The small entryway was lined with shoes, and while Nandi stopped to remove her sandals, I kept my running shoes on. This was not a time for niceties. The screams were deafening and coming from a room directly to the right of us. A young boy was sitting in front of the closed door. He stood up when he saw us.

"What are you doing here?" he asked belligerently.

"Get out the way, Sandeep, "Nandi said. "We are here to see your sister."

"She is being taken care of," he said, not moving. Nandi made it look like she would slap him, but I grabbed her upraised hand.

"Sandeep," I said. "I'm the new doctor. ...."

"And you will let us through, young man," a firm voice said behind me.

I turned to see a petite woman standing behind me, dressed in a brown nun's dress and wimple.

Nandi bowed and said respectfully, "Mother, you are here too."

The nun nodded and looked at me momentarily before asking, "You are the new doctor?"

I nodded. I looked at Sandeep, who had not moved away from the door.

"Sandeep, we are here to help your sister," the nun said persuasively. "Let us through, son."

Sandeep looked at our faces, indecision clearly written on his young face. The nun smiled at him, and he slowly moved away from the entrance.

During our exchange, the screaming had stopped. I pushed open the door and walked into a bizarre scene. A metal-framed bed was pushed to the center of the room, and I could clearly see the skid marks on the cement floor where it had been moved. A young woman was on the bed, her arms held down by two women. Her legs were held down by a man. She was tossing her head from side to side, and I could see foam on the edge of her lips. She was moaning softly. At the head of the bed was a tall and imposing figure of a woman. Her hair streamed around her face and shoulders in tangled knots. She wore a bright-colored skirt and a piece of cloth around her chest. Her chest and arms were covered in intricate tattoo marks, making her dusky skin seem even darker. She wore large earrings and had a round gold nose ring that glittered in the light of the overhead light bulb dangling from an electrical cord. The woman looked at me and then the nun, amusement clearly written on her face. I was so shocked at the entire scene that I froze for a long moment. The nun touched my shoulder, and she gave me a gentle push forward toward the bed.

"Your help is not needed," the man spoke first. "Bhadra Ma is taking care of my daughter."

"Your daughter seems to be having an epileptic seizure," I said. My voice sounded squeaky, and I straightened my shoulders, unconsciously mimicking my mother's gesture. At the thought of my mother, I felt my courage and training kicking in. I moved to the side of the bed and knelt by the young woman's side. Her eyes were unfocused, and then she started to tremble and shake.

I laid my hand on her shoulder and looked at the woman nearest me.

"Please, I can help her."

The woman looked up at Bhadra, who nodded and said softly, "Let the doctor help Indra."

The woman moved aside, and I turned the girl on her side and waved everyone away from her. A few minutes later, her seizure stopped and she opened her eyes.

"Indra," I said. "My name is Dr. Sunny and I want to give you some medicine. Do you understand?"

The girl nodded even though she looked a bit confused. I took out an anti-seizure pill. A woman quickly appeared at my side with a tumbler of water. The girl swallowed the pill and lay back down.

The nun had stayed silent and supportive throughout this visit. Still, she walked around the bed and stood directly before Bhadra. I looked closely at Bhadra's attractive face for the first time. She had a slim and straight nose with high cheekbones and full lips. Her teeth were very white against her dark skin.

"What were you doing, Bhadra?" the nun asked quietly. "I thought we had an understanding."

"Mother, let's go outside and talk," Bhadra said. Her voice was deep.

I sat by my patient. She looked so young.

The girl's mother sat down beside me on the cement floor.

"Doctor," she said. "Thank you for coming."

I nodded and said, "Epilepsy is hard on the patient and especially on loved ones watching an episode. There are medicines to help with this condition. How long has she been like this?"

"She started having these fits a few months ago. We didn't know what to do. So, we...."

"You called Bhadra to help?"

She looked at me in surprise and said, "No, no. We consulted a medicine man from a different village because we didn't want our neighbors to know about Indra's condition. He said she had a demon growing inside her, and we needed to drive it out."

She paused. I turned my head and looked at her. Tears were running down her face, and I couldn't help feeling sorry for her. I placed my right hand over hers. She squeezed my fingers and wiped her face with her sari.

"How did you drive out the demon?" I asked, fearing the worst.

"He told us to use a special switch to beat the demon out of her. My husband held her down, and I beat her legs with the switch. It seemed to help, and she stopped having them. But then the fits began again, and they were more intense than before. We called the medicine man, and he told us we had to take more drastic actions to drive out the demon. He was here this morning and told us...."

She became distraught and started to sob. I let her weep. Finally, she stopped.

"He told us the next time she had a fit; we would have to burn the demon out of her. I couldn't imagine doing this to my baby girl. That's when I sent Babu to bring Bhadra here. She kept us calm and sat with Indra as she had fit after fit, and when she started to foam at the mouth, Bhadra thought it was time we got more help. She told us to get the new village doctor, and I sent Babu to your clinic."

I was surprised at this information. Bhadra was turning out to be a very mysterious woman.

I stood up, and Indra's mother also got up.

"She looks like she is going to be fine for now. Come to the clinic tomorrow, and I'll give her a thorough examination," I said to her.

I walked outside to find my mother talking to the nun and Bhadra.

"Ah, there you are," my mother said proudly. "This is my daughter, the new village doctor."

The nun looked at me with serious eyes. Her intense grey eyes seemed to be looking inside my head.

"I'm pleased to meet you, Doctor?"

"My name is Sunny," I said.

I could see a twinkle of amusement in her eyes, and I couldn't help liking her.

"I'm Mother Superior of the Carmelite mission, a short distance from here. We have a small clinic and have always worked closely with the village doctor. The sisters at the mission are skilled at nursing, and we have a few beds for patients who need special care. You should visit the mission."

"Thank you, Mother," I said. "I would love to visit and thank you for your help back there."

"You seemed to have it in hand," she replied. "I must be getting back now. Little Mother, it was good to finally meet you. Stop by the mission the next time you are visiting Dr. Sunny, and we can share a cup of tea."

She then turned and walked down the hill. I turned to my mother and Bhadra, who was watching me.

"You have the healing touch, Dr. Sunny," Bhadra told me. She grabbed my right hand and studied my palm for a long moment. "Ah, I can see that your destiny lies in these hills. You will find joy and pain."

I pulled my hand away and moved away from the woman or witch or whatever she was. She vaguely reminded me of my sister's gypsy friend Priya, who told fortunes and read palms. But there was something inexplicable about this woman with her easy smile and knowing eyes.

My mother saw my unease and moved closer to me.

"Bhadra, you know how I feel about fortune-telling," she said.

I looked at my mother. Did she know Bhadra?

"Ah, Little Mother," Bhadra said, a teasing note in her voice. "But this is not fortune-telling. It is future-telling. I see what I see."

"Thangam, we need to get back. You have a busy day tomorrow getting ready to open the clinic. Come on."

We started walking up the hill back to the clinic when my mother stopped me with a hand on my arm.

"Wait here, Thangam," she said and hurried back to where Bhadra was still standing, watching us with glittering eyes.

Bhadra bent down and nodded as my mother said something to her. She nodded once more before walking away.

"What was that all about, Amma?"

"Nothing, Thangam."

"What do you know about her, Amma?"

My mother said, "Bhadra believes she is a direct descendant of the goddess who was said to have founded Mahagiri. Her unique healing powers make her something of a frightening figure, so villagers call her a witch. I think she will be a great help to you, Thangam."

This surprised me and I had more questions, but they would have to wait because we had arrived at the clinic.

We found Nandi waiting by the jeep. She invited my mother to stay for dinner, but my mother was impatient to go home.

"Thangam, you know you can call me any time you want," she said as she hugged me hard.

The cell phones worked sporadically here, but I promised her I would.

"When you have a quiet day, come for lunch or dinner," she said.

She climbed into the jeep, and Jaibal gave one last honk of the car horn before disappearing down the hillside. I sighed and turned toward my room. My mother's furniture had made this space welcoming and cozy.

In a corner was a water dispenser and a clay pot filled with cool well water. A steel cup was on top of the dispenser. I filled the cup and placed it on the table.

"Dr. Sunny, you must be hungry. May I serve you dinner?"

I nodded and said, "Thank you, Nandi."

I wanted to ask if she was going to join me. I didn't want to invite her because I was looking forward to some alone time.

As if she could read my mind, she said, "Please eat while everything is hot. Just place the dirty plates outside. I'll send Kamala to get them."

Kamala was her teenage daughter. I walked into the washroom at the back of the house. It had an indoor toilet and a sink. There was a cold-water tap, and Nandi had agreed to bring hot water whenever I needed to bathe. I washed my hands and face and ate my solitary meal. Unlike my older sister, Meena, I was not a cook. I appreciated good food because my mother, Devi, and Meena had always provided enticing and delicious meals. In college, I had to make do with whatever the cafeteria provided. I wasn't a fussy eater and usually ate to fill my stomach.

I lifted the steel top off the plate and found an appetizing meal. There was hot rice, a steaming stew of beans and potatoes, and a vegetable dish made of cabbage. Dessert was a small container of sticky rice pudding, fragrant with jaggery and ghee. I was hungry, and I cleaned the plate and washed everything down with several cups of well water. Mahagiri water has a unique flavor. It was cold and crisp with a tang of mineral. I missed this thirst-quenching liquid while attending college and was happy to drink it again.

After brushing my teeth, I laid out clothes for the morning and my white doctor's coat. I was glad to slip into the clean sheets. The bed reminded me of my mother. I was grateful she had gone to the trouble to make it this morning. Even as I was thinking about my strange day, I fell asleep.

CHAPTER NINE
LINGAM'S PROMISE

A loud banging woke me up. For a moment, I was disoriented and didn't know where I was. The clock by my bedside read 5:02.

I got up and pulled a blanket from the foot of the bed. I tossed it over my shoulder and went through to the living room.

"Who's there?"

"Dr. Sunny," a voice called out. "You have to come with me. I need your help."

"Alright, wait there," I said through the closed door.

I hurried to the bedroom and pulled on jeans, a warm sweatshirt, and a scarf. I was glad of the sturdy hiking shoes my brother-in-law, Raj, had insisted I take. I grabbed my medical bag, and a man barged in as soon as I opened the door. I stepped back, a little surprised and taken off-guard.

"Sorry, Dr. Sunny," he said. "I didn't mean to frighten you. My name is Lingam, and I need your help. My son is hurt."

"Where is he?"

"At my village. I couldn't carry him, and so I came for help."

Just as I was pondering what to do, Ari walked in.

"Dr. Sunny, I saw your light was on. Oh, Lingam, why are you here?" he asked. "What's going on?"

I explained, and Ari offered to drive us. Soon, we were bouncing our way down the slope.

"Lingam lives in a small village a few kilometers from here. Going by car takes a bit longer," Ari said.

"Yes, I used the shortcut, you know, the footpath," Lingam said, his voice filled with urgency.

The air was cool on my face, and I wrapped the scarf around my head and neck. The sun was just a weak promise on the eastern horizon, and the jeep's headlights showed potholes and rocks on the road.

"Can you drive to most of the villages?" I asked Ari.

He expertly turned the wheel, avoiding a protruding rock.

"Yes, but some are only accessed on foot. There is a bus service to most of the villages. Sometimes, the bus only comes once a week."

I wondered how the villagers got their groceries. I must have said this aloud because Ari answered me.

"There is a huge market on Sundays, and all the villages come together to shop, barter, and trade," Ari said. "You should visit this Sunday."

I could see the lights of a village just ahead, lighting up the early morning gloom.

"The boy is in the stall," Lingam spoke up. He leaned over my shoulder, and I could smell the rank smell of stale toddy on his breath.

"What are you up to, Lingam?" Ari said. "You smell like a toddy distillery."

He mumbled something and sat back.

"What is a stall?"

Ari answered, "A stall starts out as a tea stand, where hot tea and snacks are served during the day, but at night, it turns into a toddy stall where alcohol is served with no snacks. We try to limit the stalls, but it is not an easy task."

I turned to look at Lingam, who glared at me with blood-shot eyes.

"Why was your son at the stall?" I asked him.

He sighed, sending out a gust of toddy-laden breath, and I leaned further back in my seat.

"I went for a drink. A man is allowed a drink, no matter what people say. I had a few drinks, and the boy came to the stall to find me. Everything else is a blur. All I remember is seeing my boy lying in a pool of blood."

"Drive faster," I said to Ari. "The boy could be in real trouble."

I didn't like the sound of this story. My mind was thinking the worst. I pressed a finger to my forehead, wishing I had a cup of caffeine.

"We are almost there," Ari said, pointing to a cluster of lights straight ahead. He stopped the jeep, and I jumped out with my bag.

"Where's the stall?" I asked Lingam.

He pointed to a building down the path, and we both started running toward it. We arrived at a well-lit hut which was a generous description of the shanty. Several men were sitting on stools and standing around. A boy lay on the dirt floor, his head resting on a wadded-up blanket.

I rushed to his side. His eyes were closed, and I gently shook him.

"What is his name?" I looked up at Lingam.

"Ganesha," he replied.

"Ganesha, Ganesha, wake up," I said.

The boy mumbled something and opened his eyes. I examined his pupils, which didn't look too dilated. That was a good sign.

"Ganesha, can you see my fingers," I asked, holding up my pointing finger.

He squinted at my raised hand and nodded.

"Do you feel sick to your stomach?"

"No," he whispered.

He had a cut on the side of his head, but the blanket seemed to have stopped the bleeding. I was worried about concussion.

"Did he lose consciousness when he fell down?" I asked, looking around at the crowd.

A man behind the makeshift counter wiped his hands on a grey piece of cloth and shook his head.

"No, Doctor, he had been awake and complaining of a headache for the past hour. He just now started to fall asleep."

I nodded. I cleaned the wound. It didn't look too deep. There was no need for stitches. I applied an anti-biotic ointment and wrapped a bandage around this head.

I sat back on my heels. "Right, it looks like he needs to go to a hospital for a full exam. He may have a concussion."

"Will he be alright?" Lingam asked, sitting down next to me.

I said nothing as I looked at the distraught father. I wanted to give him good news, but I also wanted to be cautious.

"I don't know, but he is young and healthy. If there are no internal injuries, he should be fine."

Lingam sobbed. He placed a shaking hand on the boy's chest and leaned over him.

"I promise, my boy, never to take another drink. I promise."

Ari sat on my other side and said, "Dr. Sunny, we can take the boy to the mission. Mother Superior can care for him until an ambulance arrives."

"How far is the mission from here?"

"It is just over a hill," he said.

I knew the term over the hill meant anywhere from a few to many kilometers, but I really didn't know what else I could do.

"Head injuries require rest and frequent monitoring," I said. "So, the mission is probably our best option."

Under my direction, the men carried Ganesha using a large blanket as a makeshift stretcher.

"Careful," I said as they placed the youngster in the back seat. I sat beside the boy, keeping him as still and stable as possible.

"Let's go, Ari," I ordered.

"Can I come too, Dr. Sunny?" Lingam asked.

I looked at Ari before answering.

"I suppose they will need his father to sign him in," I said. "Come on, Lingam."

He gave me a grateful smile and climbed into the passenger seat.

Ari drove carefully, but it was still a bumpy ride. This time, over the hill, was just a short ride, and we soon arrived at the mission. The mission comprised several buildings, all behind a high wall. Mother Superior was propping open the gates as we drove up. Behind the nun, I could make out a courtyard filled with plants, flowers, and a fountain.

"Dr. Sunny, Ari. What's going on?"

I spoke up. "This boy has a bad head injury. I think he might be concussed. He needs to go to the hospital for further tests. Can he wait here, Mother?"

"I'll call for an ambulance," the nun said. "Ari, you and Lingam take the boy to the hospital wing."

She turned to a novice standing by the gate and gave her some instructions. The nun then looked at me and said, "Dr. Sunny, come and have a cup of hot tea."

"Thank you," I smiled at her. "But first, let me make sure Ganesha is settled in."

"I understand. Go to the end of courtyard and you'll see the open door."

"Thank you," I said again and started down the tidy stone pathway. I paused. "Did you say you have a telephone? A landline?"

"Yes. Cell phones are not always dependable here."
I nodded and turned down the path. I found the door to the clinic open. There was a large waiting area and several smaller rooms. I followed the sound of voices and found Ganesha on a clean cot. A nun was giving him a drink from a cup. She looked up and smiled at me.

"Dr. Sunny. I hope you don't mind. The boy was thirsty, and I had some cool jeera water."

"That is perfect," I said. "My nanny used to say jeera water was the best drink for any ailment."

The boy lay back down, and I bent over him. He looked much more alert.

"Does your head hurt, Ganesha?"

"Just a little bit."

"Do you feel dizzy or nauseous?"

"No, doctor," he said in a soft voice.

I beamed at him. "That is good news. You try and rest. When the ambulance comes, we will take you to the hospital to check you out. Soon, you'll be running around again."

"Thank you, Dr. Sunny."

"Dr. Sunny, can I stay here with my boy?" Lingam asked.

I looked at the sister. This was her clinic. She smiled and said, "Of course. There is an army cot, and you can sleep on it next to your son."

Ari walked outside with me. I found Mother Superior.

"Has the boy settled in?" she asked me.

"Yes, he is resting, and his father is with him."

"Good, good. Can you join me for tea and breakfast?

"We are happy to," I said, turning to Ari with a questioning look.

"I'll go to the kitchen," he said. "You can find me there or at the front gate when you are finished."

I nodded and followed the nun.

"We don't allow visitors into our inner cloister, but they are welcome in the parlor," she said, leading me into an inviting room filled with a comfortable sofa and a small dining table. There were four chairs around the highly polished table. One wall was filled with bookshelves. Against another wall was a long table covered with a lacy tablecloth with several serving plates and large bowls on it. The room was warm from the fireplace.

"Please sit down," she said, indicating the sofa. She sat in another chair opposite me and close to the burning log fire.

"Thank you," I said, looking around the room. "I didn't think I'd see you so soon. This is an inviting space."

The older woman smiled and said, "We are glad to help. Our mission is straightforward. We take care of anyone who is sick or needs our help. Even though we live a cloistered life, I like to have this area open to visitors."

"How long have you been here?"

She was about to answer when the door opened, and a woman carrying a tea tray entered.

"Ah, Girija, thank you. You can put the tray on the table and I'll pour it."

The nun turned to look at me. "This is Girija. She just joined my staff a few months ago. She is a talented cook."

The woman wore a bright green sari with the end draped over her head. She moved the end to cover her face and nodded at me. She had thin, almost bird-like hands and fingers. I caught a glimpse of a large gold nose ring.

"Do you need anything else, Mother?" she asked softly.

"Thank you, Girija."

She waited until the woman left the room to get up and pour me a cup of tea.

"Milk and sugar?"

"Just milk," I said.

The tea was strong and hot. I took a sip and felt the caffeine doing its magic. I sighed.

"To answer your question, Dr. Sunny," Mother said.

"I came to India more than 35 years ago. I was posted in a tiny nunnery in Kerala. When this mission opened about 25 years ago, I came here with a small group of women. I have been living in Mahagiri since then."

She paused to sip the tea.

"Oh, I forgot to offer you some bread," she said, gesturing toward the tray. "The bread is made in our kitchen with grains we grind in our mill, and the honey is from the hives in our garden."

I took a bite of the brown toast, spread with a thin layer of golden honey.

"Oh, this tastes like lavender," I said. "It's delicious."

Mother smiled. "I'm impressed you can taste the flavor."

"I grew up around people who were extraordinary cooks. I can't cook, but I can taste and appreciate flavors."

"How are you settling in?"

I finished the last bite of toast and took a sip of tea before replying.

"This is my first day; it has been an early start. Ari and Nandi are very generous. She has been making my meals and this morning, Ari drove me to the village to treat the injured boy. But I need to look into getting my own jeep."

"Hmm," she said, putting her cup and saucer on the tray. "Would you like some more tea?"

"Yes, please," I got up and held out my cup.

"I have a somewhat radical idea if you are interested," she said, watching me with her calm grey eyes.

"I like radical ideas," I said. "Even though I'm not radical. In my family, my mother and sister are the radicals."

"Your mother is not radical," she smiled at me. "She is an original thinker. And, Dr. Sunny, I think you might be, too," she said, wagging a finger at me. "You just haven't found your feet yet. Give it time.

"Now, about my idea, Girija is a wonderful chef and recently married Ragu, a retired police constable. Ragu grew up in our mission, and when he returned a year ago, he met Girija and fell in love with her. Now, I'm thinking you should take them on."

I put down the cup and saucer on the side table. This was unexpected.

"Mother, Nandi has already agreed to cook my meals," I began.

The older woman held up her hand to interrupt me.

"Did you have white rice, a stew of potatoes and cabbage, and perhaps some sticky rice pudding?"

I looked at her in astonishment.

"How did you know?"

She chuckled. "I know because that is all Nandi can make. You will have that meal for the next 20 years."

"Oh," I said. "It tasted good last night."

"I'm sure you will enjoy it for a few days, maybe even a week or two, but you will get tired soon enough. Girija is a talented cook, and she will do all the housework. Ragu is a dependable man who can repair and build anything. He can drive you in his jeep."

"He has a jeep?" I asked.

"Yes, it belongs to the mission, but it will be more useful for you. The villages are spread out, and you will need a reliable vehicle and driver."

I remembered how Lingam's toddy breath and wild manner had frightened me this morning. It would be nice to have someone to answer the door at night and drive me on calls.

"Mother, I agree it's a good idea. I need to talk to Ari about it because it is, after all, his bungalow."

"Actually, that building belongs to the mission," she said. "We lease it to the government as housing for the village doctor."

My salary was paid by the government hospital and now remembered Dr. Balakrishnan mentioning the hospital provided my housing. It all made sense now.

I thought for a long moment and then smiled at the nun. "Alright, that sounds like a plan."

"Good, good," she said, standing up. "Come along, let's talk to Ari, and then I'll introduce you to Ragu."

Ragu turned out to be a stalky bald man with massive arms and a scary look until he smiled. Then he looked like a giant, bald teddy bear.

"Dr. Sunny," he said, taking my hand in his substantial paw-like hands. "Everyone is talking about you."

I blushed. "I'm the new attraction right now."

"Now, Ragu, Dr. Sunny, and I've discussed the idea of you and Girija helping her," the Mother Superior said.

He let go of my hand and turned toward the nun. "We would be honored to take on this job," he said, his manner a bit formal and stiff. He bowed slightly and said excitedly, "I'll go tell Girija."

Ari just then walked into the courtyard.

"Ah, Ragu, how long will it take for you to get ready?" the Mother Superior asked.

"A few hours, Mother," he replied. "We have only a few things."

"Ari," the nun addressed the head man. "Why don't you go back home? Ragu will bring Dr. Sunny."

"I'll walk you to the car, Ari," I said. As soon as we were out of earshot, I touched his forearm and forced him to stop. "Listen, Ari, I don't know how it happened, but the Mother Superior has asked me to take on Ragu as my driver and Girija to help around the house."

I needn't have worried that this news would upset Ari, who smiled delightedly and said, "That is wonderful. Nandi and I were wondering how long I could keep driving you, and I really didn't like the idea of you being by yourself in the clinic."

Slightly surprised at how quickly things had changed, I returned to where the Mother Superior was waiting for me. She gave me a short tour of the garden. I admired the herbs, the beautiful flowers, and the white wooden boxes filled with buzzing bees. There was a large outdoor oven for baking bread and, in the back, a stone mill for grinding grain into flour. The kitchen was spotless, and the shelves were filled with jars of preserved fruit, vegetables, and pickles.

Ari and Girija were ready in no time, and the three of us soon bounced along in a large and exceptionally clean jeep. Girija sat in the back, surrounded by cloth bags of clothes and some pots and pans.

CHAPTER TEN
CLINIC OPENING

I arrived at the clinic to find a group of people waiting outside. Ragu turned and looked at me. He nodded toward the group.

"Dr. Sunny, take care of your patients. Girija and I will let ourselves in."

"Are you sure?"

"We are sure," Girija said. "Go and do your job."

She said this so kindly; I didn't feel she was bossing me around. She vaguely reminded me of my mother, who had a way of getting us to do what she wanted. I would have to keep a sharp eye on her.

I entered the clinic through the living room and closed the door behind me. I turned on the lights and looked around. Everything looked tidy and neat.

I walked to the narrow front hall that served as the waiting room. I unlocked the front doors, and a stream of patients entered and found places to sit. There was a bit of shuffling and scraping of chairs as people settled down.

I placed a clipboard on the table; the pencil was attached to it with a piece of jute string. I looked around at the faces, some in obvious pain and others with resigned looks.

"Alright, is anyone bleeding?"

No one answered.

"Is anyone vomiting or having diarrhea?"

One person, a plump young woman, raised her hand.

"Okay, miss, I need you to come to the table and write down your name."

"Who has a fever or headache?"

An old man raised his hand and coughed into his palm. He sounded very congested.

"You, sir, are next. Please print your name and sit down. After he is done, everyone else can print their names on the clipboard."

I went up to the clipboard and glanced down.

"Yamuna? Please come with me."

I lead the young woman into the examination room. I placed a file on the side table and wrote "Patient #003" on the tab. I considered Indra and Ganesha to be the first two patients.

"Please sit on the table," I told Yamuna, taking a seat on the stool.

"What is your full name?"

"Yamuna Jogi," she said. "I'm married to Jogi Gowder."

I wrote all this down, as well as her age and symptoms, which included vomiting and feeling nauseous.

"When did you have your last bleeding?"

The girl thought about it and shook her head before replying. "I don't remember."

"Are you and Jogi trying to have a baby?"

The girl's eyes widened, and she said. "Yes, but it is bad luck to keep wishing for one. The medicine man in my village told me so."

This medicine man was talking to a lot of my patients. One of these days, I would have to pay him a visit.

"When did you and Jogi sleep together as a man and woman," I asked, trying to be as sensitive as possible. I sensed Yamuna would run out of the room if we talked about sex or intercourse.

"Every night," she said in a matter-of-fact tone. "My husband says I must please him every night."

I paused. I cleared my throat to give myself a moment to think of what to say next. They didn't teach us about such situations in medical college.

"Do you want to do it every night?"

"Well, sometimes I'm tired after all the housework and would just like to sleep," she said shyly.

I listened to her heart and lungs. Everything seemed normal.

I walked over to the cupboard and removed a plastic cup with a lid. I wrote Yamuna's name on it and handed it to her. I realized there was no place for her to go to the bathroom. She would have to use my personal bathroom. I went out into the hallway.

"Girija," I called out.

The woman came out the kitchen with an enquiring look on her face.

"Yamuna needs to use the latrine. Can you show her the way to my bathroom?"

I turned to Yamuna, "Use this cup and fill it halfway with urine and then put the lid on it."

"She can use the latrine in the back," Girija said.

I nodded; a bit relieved that patients didn't have to go into my private quarters.

I finished filling out the information from my conversation. I looked up when Yamuna came back into the exam room with a cup in one hand.

I said, "Alright, Yamuna, I'm going to send this urine to the hospital for testing, and I want you to come back in a week to see me again. Meanwhile, I want you to drink ginger tea whenever you feel sick. Keep a salty biscuit or *varki* by your bedside, and before you get out of bed, I want you to nibble on the salty biscuit. Then, when you get up, drink some ginger tea. Prepare the tea in the evening and let the ginger seep in warm water so it is strong."

I looked at her eager face. "Also, I'm writing you a note to give your husband. Can he read English?"

"Oh, yes, Dr. Sunny. He went to college."

In my neatest handwriting, I wrote: *"Mr. Gowder. Your wife needs to rest and sleep for the next week. She should not engage in any sexual activity. After I examine her next Thursday, I will let you know how she is doing." Signed Dr. Sunny.*

I wasn't sure this would help, but I needed to do something.

I led her outside and called in the next person. For the next few hours, I was busy seeing patients with chronic arthritis, a terrible cold and cough, a child with tapeworm, and another with diarrhea. I had small samples of medicine to give them. Since the nearest pharmacy was in Lower Mahagiri, I had to find a way to get medications for my patients. Mother Superior may have some suggestions.

When I visited the Mahagiri Government Hospital, I was assured by the director that I would get everything I needed. I remember that the hospital arranged with the bus company to transport blood and other specimens from the clinic to the hospital for further analysis. I also needed to get my computer up and running. Results could be faster if they were emailed to me. But I still had more patients to see before I could do that. I was about to call the next person in when Ragu walked in with a bunch of bananas in his arms. He winked at me and walked out into the waiting room. I followed him to see him hand out a banana to each person in the waiting room and tell them they needed to go outside and eat the fruit.

I was about to protest, but he shook his head and said, "Dr. Sunny, you have been working for over six hours with no break. You must come and have lunch, drink some tea, and sit down for thirty minutes. Your patients will still be here."

He closed and locked the clinic door, and we walked into the living room. I was surprised to see the wooden table covered with a white linen cloth and a vase of wildflowers in the middle. A plate filled with thick slices of bread, tomato, cucumber, and greens was waiting for me.

I went to the bathroom and washed my hands.

"Dr. Sunny, you can make a sandwich with the vegetables. I have my secret sauce for you to spread on the bread," Girija said, pushing a bowl filled with a creamy sauce toward me.

I sat down, spread the garlicky sauce on a slice of bread, and topped it with slices of tomatoes, cucumber, and a small handful of greens. I took a huge bite of the thick sandwich. My mouth exploded with the flavor of garlic, peppery greens, juicy tomatoes, and crisp cucumbers. I groaned aloud at the deliciousness of it all.

"This is so good, Girija," I said after I swallowed my first bite. "What is the green stuff?"

"That is watercress from the mission garden. Mother Superior gave me some fresh produce."

I finished the sandwich and drank a glass of water.

"Would you like some tea?" Girija asked.

The tea was hot and just what I needed. I felt so refreshed I wanted to rush back into the clinic. But I knew the couple required attention, so I sat back in my chair with the tea cup and looked at them. They were both standing near the doorway.

"Come and sit down," I said, pointing to the bench.

Ragu shook his head and said, "That's all right, Dr. Sunny. We are enjoying watching you eat. Would you like to see what we have been doing?"

I put the cup down, pushed the chair back, and followed the couple into the kitchen. When I had first seen this kitchen, it had been dark and dank. I had shuddered at the thought of cooking or eating in here. Now, I gasped at the transformation. The tar paper covering the windows had been ripped off, and the room was filled with light. The concrete floor was sparkling clean. There was an old-fashioned hearth fueled by wood. A two-burner gas stove was also connected to a red gas cylinder on the ground. The shelves had all been scrubbed, and a few pots and pans were on them.

"The larder still needs to be cleaned and filled," Girija said, pointing to a small space.

"Where will you sleep?"

"We are cleaning out the storage room next door," Ragu said. "There is a space to clean dishes in the back, and I'll build a shelter there for us to bathe."

I was overwhelmed at how much these two had done in such a short time. They must have worked hard.

"I hope I don't have to remind the two of you to have lunch?" I said in a teasing voice.

Girija laughed and said, "No, no. We'll take care of ourselves. Do you need anything else?"

"I'm full and happy," I said with a grin. "And now I'm ready to tackle more patients.

"Ragu, before I forget, can you come by the clinic around five and pick up some lab samples? They need to be on the 5:30 bus to

Lower Mahagiri. The hospital has made arrangements with the driver and conductor."

CHAPTER ELEVEN

INDRA

The last patient had just left and I was completing patient notes when I heard the front door of the clinic being opened. Another patient? I sighed to myself. I had thought I was done for the day. It was nearly seven.

I walked into the waiting area and found Indra and her mother.

"Indra," I greeted her. "Are you feeling better?"

The girl nodded shyly. "I'm better."

I turned to her mother and asked, "What did the hospital staff say? Did they prescribe any medication?"

The woman looked sheepish as I invited them into the examination room. After they were seated, she looked up at me.

"Please, you have to understand, Dr. Sunny, I couldn't take Indra to the hospital. She took the medicine you gave her and felt much better."

"Indra needs to be fully tested," I said.

"Can't you just give her some more medicine?" the woman asked.

I shook my head as I looked over at Indra. The situation was getting frustrating.

"Amma," she said. "I need to go to the latrine."

"The latrines are in the back," I said. "Let me call Girija."

I walked to the living room and called for Girija, who appeared immediately.

"Yes? Dr. Sunny, are you done for the day?"

"No, I have a patient who needs to use the latrine," I said. "Can you show her the way?"

While Girija accompanied Indra, I went back to the exam room. Her mother looked agitated.

"Dr. Sunny, the girl has a bladder the size of a pea. She always gets up to go to the bathroom, even in the middle of the night. I tell her not to drink so much water, but she is always thirsty."

I had read in some medical journals that epilepsy and diabetes were linked. *Could Indra have diabetes or pre-diabetes?*

When Indra returned, I asked her to sit on the exam table.

"I'm going to draw some blood," I told her. "I want to run some tests, which could help us determine what is going on with you."

After I finished, I labeled the test tube, ready to go out on tomorrow's bus.

"Meanwhile, I want Indra to limit sugar," I said. "No more sugar in tea or coffee. No sweets or starch, either. Instead of white rice, have ragi with spinach and dal."

After they left, I sat in the empty examination room. My first day had been exhausting, but I was filled with quiet joy. I felt at home here in this little clinic. Tomorrow, I will visit the mission and talk to Mother Superior about how to address my patients' emotional and psychological welfare. I wanted to be ready to handle all their needs.

I ensured the medicine cabinet and front door were locked before turning off the lights. The kitchen smelled delicious. I followed the sound of voices back to the storage room, where I found the couple. Again, I was amazed at the transformation of the formerly dingy space. They had cleaned, dusted, and cleared out the room. There was no furniture in the room yet, and several wicker baskets served as an open dresser filled with folded clothes. A pile of blankets and two pillows were at the foot of a bamboo mat, ready to be made into a makeshift bed on the floor.

"This looks amazing," I said to them. They both stopped talking and looked at me, a little embarrassed.

"You need some furniture and a bed," I told them.

"Oh, Dr. Sunny, I hoped to show you the room when it was all done. I must still make up my pooja table and hang some pictures."

Ragu laughed. "Dr. Sunny, when she says some pictures, don't believe her. The entire wall will be filled with pictures."

I backed out of the room with a smile and said, "I look forward to seeing them."

Girija followed me and said, "I have hot water here if you want to take a bath before dinner."

"That would be perfect," I said. "After dealing with patients all day, I could use a good wash."

Ragu had brought a tin bucket of hot water to the bathroom. I used a plastic bucket to mix cold and warm water to wash myself. It was an inefficient way to wash up, and this was the first time I had taken this kind of old-fashioned bath since I was a young child. All the plumbing in my mother's house had been updated with showers and hot and cold water. I pulled on comfortable sweats and a warm pullover and entered the living room. Girija came in with a plate of food. There was soft chapatti bread, a dal dish loaded with green onions and cumin, yogurt, and sautéed beets with garlic.

"Everything looks delicious," I said to Girija, hovering by the doorway. "Have you had your dinner yet?"

"We will eat after you finish," Girija said.

I knew they wouldn't be comfortable eating with me, but one day perhaps they would eat with me.

Ragu joined Girija in the doorway. He looked nervous, which was unlike his usual tough-man persona.

"Dr. Sunny," he said in a hesitant voice. "I was wondering if I could make a few changes around the house."

I nodded encouragingly because my mouth was full of garlicky beets and chapatti.

"Well, first, I would like to build a latrine in the exam room. The drains are already in place, so patients won't have to come through the house."

"That's a great idea," I said, swallowing a mouthful. "But I don't have a budget."

Ragu nodded, "The Mother Superior told me she has a small budget for the clinic and has agreed to any changes you approve of."

"I had no idea Mother would be so supportive," I said.

"She wants you to be comfortable and successful," Girija piped up.

"What else do you want to do, Ragu?"

Ragu cleared his throat before replying, "I would also like to build something to keep the living room warmer this winter. I know it's only spring right now, but in the winter, you will be glad of a warm place to sit, read, and have a meal."

Now Girija spoke up. They looked like they rehearsed their pitches, but I didn't mind.

"Dr. Sunny, I would like to start a small vegetable garden on the side and front of the house. I can get seeds and seedlings from the mission, and I'll take care of everything."

"I don't see any of this as a problem," I said. "Are you going to the mission anytime soon?"

"I was thinking of going tomorrow," Ragu said.

"Could you go in the afternoon? Then, I can come with you. I need Mother's advice."

We agreed to leave tomorrow afternoon as soon as there was a break from patients.

"And if anyone comes while you are gone, I'll tell them to come back tomorrow if it's not an emergency," Girija said.

That night, as I sat in bed, reading some medical journals and looking up symptoms and treatments for diabetes, I couldn't help being thankful for finding this village, this clinic, and Girija and Ragu. Life was looking good.

CHAPTER TWELVE

A NEW DAY

One of the first patients waiting to see me was Ganesha, accompanied by his father, Lingam.

I greeted them and ushered the pair into the exam room. Ganesha looked bright-eyed and happy. It was good to see him looking so healthy.

"Ganesha, what's going on?"

"I'm feeling fine, Dr. Sunny," he said with a huge grin, making him seem even younger than a twelve-year-old. "I'm going to school today."

I turned to Lingam. He didn't look hungover, and his eyes weren't bloodshot.

"And you, Lingam? How are you coping?"

"Dr. Sunny, the accident was my wake-up call," he said earnestly. "I have given up toddy and taken on the responsibility of the village garden.

"That's why Ganesha and I are here. We would like to thank you by planting a flower garden and vegetable garden at the clinic."

I laughed.

"What's so funny?" Lingam asked, looking a little hurt.

I shook my head. "It's not really funny. I'm laughing at the co-incidence. Only last night, Girija told me she would like to plant a vegetable garden, and here you are volunteering your services."

"It is like Lord Ganesha, himself, has blessed my doings," Lingam said seriously.

I said. "Why don't you both talk to Girija?

"But before you do, let me quickly examine Ganesha to ensure he is healing well.

Later that day, after lunch, Ragu and I set off to visit the mission. It was a beautiful day with a bright blue sky filled with puffy white clouds. I took a deep breath of the clear air. Just as we reached the top of the road that led to the mission, I called out, "Stop for a moment, Ragu."

He looked puzzled and pulled the jeep to the side of the road. I got out and walked a few feet to the top of the hill, where I could see the verdant valley below me. In the distance, there were clusters of white-washed buildings. Each was a village.

"Who lives there?" I pointed to a large estate set on a hillside.

Ragu had climbed up to stand beside me, "That estate belongs to Dorairaj," he said. "He is the largest landowner in this area."

"I've heard of him," I replied. "Didn't he take over the golf course project that my mother and the rest of the villagers shut down?"

"Yes, that is him. He knows how to get things done. There are many stories about him, some good and some not so good. He is human with his faults, but he is a powerful force in this area," Ragu said as he spit out a wad of tobacco.

Immediately, he pulled another plug from his shirt pocket and stuffed it into his mouth. I wanted to wean him off this bad habit. But for now, I held my peace.

"What is that?" I asked, pointing to an ample open space directly below us.

"That is the *maidan* where the weekly bazaar is held every Saturday from early morning to late at night."

"Oh, yes, I heard about it. We should go."

There were a lot of tiny villages in this valley.

"How do the villagers get around?" I asked in wonder.

"From here, it looks like a great distance, but many shortcuts and footpaths connect the different villages. The town bus goes to the *maidan*. A lot of villagers have televisions and computers. It's not as isolating as you might think."

"About that? Why don't we have internet connection at the clinic?"

"We do, Dr. Sunny. I asked Ari, and he said the cable repair man was supposed to come two weeks ago, but he was delayed. Ari promised you will have internet connection soon."

I nodded. A computer would help with communication. I could also email the local hospital and connect with my mother and sister.

"Shall we go?" Ragu asked.

"Yes, in a moment. I just wanted to look at this view. It's incredible, and it feels good to stretch my legs. I'm used to running."

"Dr. Sunny, we can park at the mission's entrance, and can walk the rest of the way to the building. It is about three kilometers," he said.

I smiled at him before replying, "That's a great idea."

True to his word, he stopped the vehicle at the start of the road leading to the mission. I got out and stretched. Soon, we were walking at a brisk pace to the mission. I enjoyed the fresh air and Ragu's quiet companionship so much that I was sorry to see the mission gates. I could have walked much longer and farther. As usual, the gates were wide open, an invitation to walk in. We entered the courtyard, and my nose was immediately overwhelmed with the heady fragrance of all the flowers and herbs. The buzzing bees only added to the wholesome and peaceful atmosphere. A nun was bent over a lavender bush, patiently clipping the purple stalks. When she turned around to place the cuttings in a basket, she saw us and got up.

"Oh, Ragu," she said, recognizing my companion. "Come in, come in. What are you doing here? Mother said you are now living at the clinic."

Ragu walked up to the elderly nun and picked up the basket of herbs. "Good afternoon, Sister Clarice. This is my new employer, Dr. Sunny."

The nun peered at me through thick glasses. Her eyes were intelligent and bright as she studied me. Her face was lined, and the white wimple didn't cover her grey hair.

"You look far too young to be a doctor and an employer of my friend Ragu."

I smiled. "I assure you, I'm older than I look, and Ragu is modest. He and Girija are quietly managing me, and I sometimes wonder who the employer and employee are."

The nun nodded and laughed in delight. She said, "You are wise to know when to let others take the lead. Come; let's have a cup of tea. I have a new hibiscus blend I want you to try."

We followed Sister Clarice to the parlor. Ragu put down the basket on a table.

"Can you please tell the kitchen novice to make us some hibiscus tea?"

"Of course, Sister," Ragu said.

"Also, please stop by the office and tell the Mother Superior she has a visitor."

When Ragu left, the nun turned to me and indicated I sit on the sofa. She took a seat opposite me. I had come to love this welcoming and comfortable room.

"Sunny is a pleasant name. Did your mother know you would have a good disposition when she named you?" she asked with a twinkle in her eye.

I laughed. "Oh no, Sister, my mother calls me Thangam. That's her nickname for me, and my given name is Subhalakshmi."

Sister Clarice nodded and said, "So, how did you become Dr. Sunny?"

"That is a story from my childhood," I said. "A school friend called me Sunny because of my yellow raincoat, and the name stuck."

"It suits you," the old nun said. "Sunny would be a lovely name for the clinic."

I was a little surprised at her suggestion, "Oh? I'm not sure I want to name the clinic after myself. It might not be a good idea."

"What would not be a good idea?" Mother Superior asked as she walked into the living room.

I stood up and greeted her.

"I was just telling Dr. Sunny here that the clinic needs a name, and one with Sunny in it might be just the thing," Sister Clarice said.

"That's a great idea. The clinic needs a new identity after the fiasco with old Dr. Williams"

She thought for a moment and suggested, "How about Sunshine Clinic or something like that?"

I blushed and replied, "I'm not sure, Mother."

"Just think about it. Sunshine Clinic has a nice ring, and we can have a grand opening to announce the new name."

"So, how are you getting on, Dr. Sunny?" Mother Superior asked, sitting in another chair next to the fireplace. "I understand you have been busy."

I smiled. Of course, she would know all about what was going on.

"It has been busy," I admitted. "Ragu and Girija have been immensely helpful. They are getting ready to make some improvements to the building. I hope that is all right with you."

"As a resident doctor, you have full autonomy over the clinic. We have a small fund to cover costs, and if necessary, we can apply for a grant or hold a fundraiser. What were you thinking of doing?"

"Ragu wants to build a latrine in the examination room. There is a washroom, and it would mean adding a toilet. After a patient asked to use the latrine, he thought this might be a good idea."

The Mother Superior looked at me with wise eyes and said, "I think that's a sensible investment. Ragu is correct; you can't have patients walking through your personal quarters. Also, I wanted to remind you to schedule some regular days off. If not, you will be working non-stop. I suggest you close the clinic on Saturdays since it is market day and everyone will be there. Somedays, say every second Saturday, you can hold an informal clinic at the market. On Sundays, I suggest you close completely. It is a day of rest, and as the unofficial clinic manager, I insist you take time off to recharge yourself."

"That answers my other questions," I said with a smile.

A novice entered with a tray and cups of steaming tea. I could smell the fragrant tea as soon as the young girl entered the room.

"Ahh, yes, tea," Sister Clarice said, accepting a cup. "This has mint, hibiscus, and a little rosehip."

I took a tentative sip of the warm liquid. It was delicious, fragrant, and lightly sweet.

"This is perfect," I said. "Sister Clarice, I need your advice on herbal tinctures. I think they might be helpful for some of my patients."

I saw the two nuns exchange looks, and Sister Clarice raised her eyebrows as she took another sip.

"Did I say something wrong?" I asked.

"No, no, child," Mother Superior said. "And sorry for calling you child, but you are a breath of fresh air and a delight. We never could convince Dr. Williams of the importance of herbal remedies. He thought we were old fools with our herbs and oils."

I put down the cup and sat forward to make my point and said. "Oh, but nutrition and herbs are crucial to health."

"Mother Superior," I said. "I also wanted to ask your advice about the mental health of my patients. I have taken some basic psychology classes, but I'm unsure I can give them professional advice."

The Mother Superior said nothing for a long moment. She stared at me with calm grey eyes, searching deep into my soul. I had to use all my willpower not to squirm and confess all my sins.

Finally, she said, "You continue to amaze me, Dr. Sunny. You are wise for one so young. Some doctors think they know everything after a few years of medical school. In our mission, Sister Monica is a trained psychologist and will be available to help you. Also, Sister Clarice has years of experience dealing with different kinds of people. She will be able to advise you as needed."

"And what about you, Mother Superior?" I asked. "You surely are in a position to counsel and offer advice?"

"Thank you, my dear, but my knowledge is self-taught."

"You sell yourself short, Mother," Sister Clarice said. "The doctor is right; you would be a great resource."

The Mother Superior changed the subject by asking, "Did a patient recently need help?"

"Yes, a young woman."

I went on to explain Yamuna's troubles. Both nuns listened without interrupting me.

"I can understand how it would be difficult to give her any sort of advice. Will she even listen to it, or will her husband?" Sister Clarice said, shaking her head.

"Your note might help," Mother Superior said. "But I suggest the next time she comes to see you, bring her here for a cup of tea. Tell her Sister Clarice has some tinctures to help with nausea, and we'll talk to her."

I nodded, relieved, and said, "Of course, it will depend on what the tests say."

I thought of something else and asked, "Mother, what about a vegetable garden? Girija would love to start one next to the clinic."

"Then she should," the nun said.

I told them about Lingam and how he had offered to plant a flower garden in the clinic's front yard.

"You are already changing lives and building a rapport with the villagers, Dr. Sunny," Mother Superior said. "All those stories we heard about your mother must be true, and you are a little chip off that maternal block."

She made us sound like blocks of cheese or chocolate, and I had to laugh aloud.

"Thank you, Mother Superior, for the great compliment. My mother is a force to be reckoned with."

Ragu and I took leave of the nuns, promising to return soon.

CHAPTER THIRTEEN
SATURDAY MARKET

"We'll leave early," Girija told me on Friday night when we discussed attending the Saturday market.

I hadn't realized how early until she came to wake me up before five in the morning.

"Do markets always start so early?" I asked grumpily as I accepted a hot coffee from her.

"Come on," she said with a grin. "If a patient needed you, you wouldn't think twice about getting up."

She had a point. The strong drink helped my grogginess, and a splash of icy cold water on my face woke me up.

I gathered my medical bag, writing pad, pens, and other items.

"We'll have breakfast at the market," Girija said. "A lady at the market sells the best rava idlis."

Rava idlis are little dumplings made from toasted cream of wheat, yogurt, and spices. Devi always made them on special occasions, and the promise of breakfast perked me up. I noticed Ragu had filled the back of the jeep with several items, including a folding table and chairs.

"What are those for," I asked, gesturing with my chin toward the back of the jeep.

"Some items we'll need to set up the medical tent."

Setting up the medical tent seemed like an elaborate affair, and I hoped I would have some time to explore the marketplace.

I must have dozed off because before I knew it, we had arrived at the market, which was already bustling with activity. Although the sun was barely cresting over the far horizon, the day had already begun in the marketplace. There was activity everywhere. Vendors were busy setting up makeshift tents while others spread mats and plastic tarps on the ground. Cattle, goats, sheep, and buffalo were penned on the far end of the market. This looked nothing like yesterday's empty meadow I had seen from the top of the hill. The place was brimming with people, animals, produce, and other items for sale.

"What time does the market open?" I asked Ragu as he made his way to the center of the marketplace.

"As soon as the vendors set up," he replied. "However, the livestock sales don't begin until after 10 o'clock, giving everyone time to come to the auction."

The medical tent was clearly marked with a red first-aid cross. I pulled aside the flaps and entered a relatively large space. Someone had already placed a large table and a couple of folding chairs inside the tent. A fabric divider provided some privacy to examine patients. Ragu opened the small card table and chairs he had brought and set them up at the tent's entrance. He pulled the flaps open so I could talk to patients and bring them back into the tent if more privacy was needed.

I grabbed a clipboard and sat down, but Girija pulled me by my arm.

"Let's go find Shankari's tent and get breakfast before she is swamped."

We passed vendors selling chili peppers, jaggery cubes, green beans, giant heads of cabbage, and bunches of fresh carrots with dirt still clinging to them.

"I hope you are going to stock up on all these fresh vegetables," I told Girija.

She nodded and replied, "I plan to do that. Oh, I meant to ask you about money."

I wanted to smack myself on the head. Of course, she needed money.

"Here," I said, handing her several rupee notes. "Will this be enough?"

She unfolded the money and said, "Oh, yes. This is plenty. I can give you an account of what I spent at the end of the day."

I replied, "We can sit down and work out our expenses when we get home. We can set a budget, and I can leave money in an envelope for you to use. That way, you won't have to ask me for money and don't have to tell me about every rupee you spend."

"That will be fine, Dr. Sunny," she said admiringly. "Let's go see if Shankari is ready for business."

We walked up to the vendor's tent, where several tables had been set up to seat about eight to ten people. In the dark interior of the tent, Shankari had set up another table with a portable gas stove. Something was steaming on the stovetop, and the air was fragrant with the tangy flavor of the rava idlis. Shankari turned around and exclaimed with delight when she saw Girija.

"Girija-didi," she said, "I'm so glad to see you. And this must be Dr. Sunny."

She turned toward me. "Dr. Sunny, I have heard so much about you from Shoba's mother, a dear friend of mine."

I blushed and replied, "And I've heard only delicious things about your famous rava idlis.

Shankari's helper, a young boy, served each of us three rava idlis on banana leaves with a generous scoop of coconut chutney. The leaves were on re-useable wicker plates. While Girija used her hands to scoop up the idlis and chutney, I pulled a fork and spoon from my purse. Shankari was stirring idli batter and paused to stare at me and my utensils.

"You carry a spoon in your purse?" Shankari asked.

I laughed and said, "Yes. In medical school, I just couldn't bear the idea of eating with my hands after dissection, so I started carrying around my spoon and fork. My mother then made this little washable bag to carry my utensils. I have two sets, so I always have a clean one to use when I eat out."

Shankari shook her head in disbelief.

I was used to this reaction. When people thought about my idea, most agreed it was hygienic and practical. I knew Shakari would come around, too.

The idlis were delicious and rich with cashew bits, cilantro, curry leaves, mustard seeds, ginger, turmeric, and green chilies. They were tender and tangy, filling every bite with exquisite flavor. The coconut chutney was stunningly spicy, making my eyes water.

Girija beckoned a boy carrying a tray with cups of coffee and tea.

"Dr. Sunny, would you care for something to drink?"

I picked a glass tumbler of tea and took a sip. I found the tea to be way too sweet for my taste. I turned to the boy and asked, "Can you bring me a glass of tea without sugar?"

"No sugar at all?"

"That's right," I replied.

"Alright, but no one likes tea without sugar," he said.

"I do," I replied with a laugh.

"Bring it before I finish this plate; there is a nice tip for you."

He was back within a few minutes with my tea. I paid him but he waited around wanting to watch me drink my unsweetened tea. I took a swallow and pretended to gag.

"See," he said excitedly. "I told you that you wouldn't like it."

I laughed before replying. "I was just teasing you. This tea is delicious."

I took several more sips to prove I liked my unsweetened tea, but he still looked skeptical.

I washed my utensils using water from a bucket used by customers to wash their hands and stored them back in my purse. We thanked Shankari and walked back to the medical tent.

"Let's go this way," I said. "I'd like to see what is being sold here."

On this side of the maidan, merchants had set up a pop-up store selling grains, lentils, and dried beans. Women were haggling with the vendors, and children were running around. It was a lovely scene. I wished my mother were here to enjoy it.

We made our way back to the medical tent. The sun was now higher in the eastern sky, and the day was warming up. It was a beautiful spring morning, and I was glad to be outside. An old lady was sitting on one of the chairs, waiting for me. I wiped my hands with an antiseptic cloth and draped the stethoscope around my neck before sitting down. Her complaint was a cough. She sounded like she had pneumonia. I asked her to come to the clinic on Monday.

"Meanwhile, here is a bottle of eucalyptus oil," I said, giving her a small vial that Mother Superior had thoughtfully given me on my last visit.

"Put a few drops in boiling water and then cover your head with a towel to breathe in the scented hot water. It should help with coughing. Do you have honey?'

"Oh, yes," she said. "My son-in-law brings honeycomb from the woods."

"Place some honey in a spoon and put two or three drops of eucalyptus oil on it. The honey will coat your throat, and the oil will soothe the cough. You can also make some hot lemon tea with honey. Drink it whenever you feel the urge to cough."

"Lemon tea," she smiled at me. "My mother used to make it for me, but I thought you would give me some real medicine."

I smiled back at her and replied, "I will, but first, I need to ensure the medicine I give you will help."

"The other doctor just gave us a bottle," she said, taking out a small vial and handing it to me.

The glass vial had a crude measurement taped on one side made of paper. Each zigzag represented one dose. I pulled the stopper and smelled the bottle. Alcohol fumes made my nose burn and my eyes sting. I had no idea what was in this medicine, but it contained quite a bit of alcohol.

"He charged 150 rupees for each bottle," the woman said. "It really helped me at night."

I bet. With all that alcohol, it probably put her to sleep right away.

"Ever since I stopped the medicine, I have quite a headache," the woman said in a complaining tone.

I gave her something for the headache.

"This should help," I said, watching her swallow the pills without any hesitation.

At this display of trust, I felt a rush of warm emotion in my chest. I had to uphold this trust by doing my best for these villagers.

"Dr. Sunny, you should visit our village," she said. "Many small children and women will want to meet you."

"Are they sick?"

"Some are, but most of us just want to meet you. Please come."

I promised to try. The day passed quickly; before I knew it, Girija was at my side with a cup of hot tea. She handed me a package tied with string.

"What is this?" I asked as I pulled off the string.

"Your lunch. Aren't you hungry?"

Inside the package was a banana leaf wrapped around a thick piece of bread filled with savory potatoes and peas. The delicious smell reminded me I hadn't eaten anything for several hours. I wiped my hands with a sanitizing wipe and bit into the tasty sandwich.

"That was perfect, Girija," I said. "You are right; I had forgotten how hungry I was. Thank you."

Girija nodded and watched me take a sip of tea.

"No sugar," she said.

I laughed and said, "Thanks for remembering."

"Actually, it was the tea boy who remembered."

I used the public restroom, which made me shudder. I was reminded of my sister Meena's aversion to public latrines, and I couldn't blame her.

Soon, Ragu started packing up.

"Time to go home, Dr. Sunny," Ragu said. "I'll bring the chairs and table."

Girija sat in the back, between bags of grain, a bunch of bananas, and many baskets and cloth bags.

Once we reached the clinic, I left the couple to unload the produce. I went to write up the notes from the patients I had seen at the market clinic. I had talked to several people but had only seen twelve patients, so I made charts for each. I had just finished the last of them when Ragu came in.

"Dr. Sunny," he said. "The Mother Superior has asked me to help at the mission tomorrow. Will that be all right?"

"Of course," I said. "The clinic is closed, and if there is an emergency, I will ask Ari to drive me. What are you doing at the mission?"

"She wants me to move some things from the store room."

Dinner was a feast made from the fresh produce Girija had bought. There was a *Dal*, rich with fenugreek greens and golden ghee. A potato and green bean stew flavored with freshly grated coconut and nutty mustard seeds. There was rice and crispy hot bread to accompany all the vegetables. For dessert, she served a plate of fruit. There were slices of green apples, the first yellow plum of the season, and a handful of wild guavas.

"Tea in a bit?" she asked.

"After you and Ragu finish your dinner," I replied.

CHAPTER FOURTEEN
REST DAY

I slept in and woke up feeling refreshed. I wandered into the kitchen to find Girija stirring something on the stove. The kitchen was filled with the tantalizing scent of frying onions, making my mouth water.

She turned around and when she saw me she said, "I was just about to come and check on you."

She handed me a cup of hot coffee. Where did that come from and so quickly?

"I had it warming on the stove by the pot of hot bath water," she replied.

I realized I must have spoken aloud.

I sipped the hot liquid and looked at her, "So, Ragu has gone to the mission?"

Girija nodded as she worked on forming lacy *dosa* (a rice crepe) on the iron griddle. She drizzled melted ghee over the crepe.

She flipped the savory crepe and the aroma of the crispy dosa filled the kitchen.

"Why don't you sit down, and I'll bring you breakfast," she said.

The *dosa* stuffed with potatoes and the spicy tomato chutney were delicious. I had three and another cup of strong coffee.

"That was beyond delicious," I said, sitting back in my chair. "Where did you learn to cook like this?"

She smiled at me.

"I've always been a good cook," Girija replied.

"Then, you are like my sister Meena, who was born to cook. Me, I can't even boil water," I said with a laugh. "Of course, I forgot to turn on the stove."

Girija laughed. "I'm sure a smart girl like you can figure anything out," she said.

I shook my head, replying, "It was easier to let Meena lead the way. My twin brother Appu liked to play sports, but I spent most of my childhood following Meena or reading."

"That sounds like a wonderful childhood," Girija said. "If you've had enough coffee, I'll go work in the garden."

It was a beautiful morning, and I was happy to be outside. I dragged a rickety-old chair I found on the side of the house and sat in the sunshine. I had some medical journals to look at, but it was so quiet and peaceful I just sat there watching Girija digging the soil.

"Didn't Lingam say he would help with this work?"

She lifted her head and replied, "Yes, but I thought I'd get started."

The peace was shattered by a sudden commotion across the way toward the village square. The clinic was located at the farthest edge of the village. The central part of the village, which included a temple, Ari's house, and the bus stop, was a short walk from the clinic. I could see something was going on near the bus stop, but I couldn't make out exactly what.

"I better go see what the fuss is all about," I said as I pushed back my chair. "I wonder if I should take my medical bag."

"Dr. Sunny, please don't get involved," Girija said. "A crowd can get ugly fast.

I turned to look at Girija, who was clearly agitated and terrified.

"Girija, I'm the village doctor," I said. "I have to see if I can help. Besides, it's daytime, and I can see Ari."

Girija didn't say anything at first but reluctantly offered to accompany me.

I shook my head and walked into the house to pick up my medical bag and put on some walking shoes before heading toward the small crowd at the foot of the large jacaranda tree.

"Ari," I called out. "What's going on?"

The headman ran toward me and put a hand on my arm.

"Oh, Dr. Sunny, I'm glad to see you. I was just about to get you. We need your help. Something terrible has happened."

CHAPTER FIFTEEN
INJURED GIRL

I followed Ari to the bus stop, and when he pushed people aside, I saw a young woman, who looked incredibly young, lying on the ground. I gently turned her onto her back and gasped at the mass of bruises on her face. Her eyes were swollen shut. Her jaw had an angry red mark, and her arm was dangling at an odd angle. She had a thready pulse, and her breathing was noisy and labored because of a broken or damaged nose. I ran my hands gently over her legs and hips. I would have to do a more thorough exam to comprehend the full extent of her injuries.

I sat back on my heels and looked up at the men, and a couple of women gathered around us.

"What happened? Who is this girl?"

No one answered, and I turned to Ari.

"What is going on?"

He came and squatted beside me and heaved a heavy sigh.

"I wish I knew, Dr. Sunny. Balu, who was coming to get the noonday bus, saw what he thought was a bundle of rags on the side of the road. When he came closer, he saw it was this injured girl, and he immediately came to get me."

I looked at the crowd and wondered how everyone else had heard this news. But right now, my main concern was the patient.

"I need you to go to the clinic, Ari, and bring the stretcher. Girija knows where it is stored. I need to assess her injuries and determine if we should take her to the mission or the hospital."

The girl on the ground stirred and whimpered. She struggled to open her eyes.

"Shh," I said. "Stay still. My name is Dr. Sunny and I'll take care of you at my clinic, where you will be safe."

She mumbled something, and I leaned down and asked her, "What?"

"No hospital," she whispered. I could barely make out her words.

Ari and Balu came back with the stretcher and a cotton blanket. I spread the blanket on the stretcher, and under my direction, we transferred the injured girl onto the blanket.

Ari directed some of the men to help lift the stretcher.

We must have made an odd procession.

"Through the clinic entrance," I said, pointing to the door. "Please gently place her on the exam table."

I had two men hold the stretcher while the other two used the blanket to transfer the girl onto the exam table.

They did what I asked, and the young woman groaned softly.

"Everyone, clear out," I yelled.

I turned to Ari and said, "You, as the village headman, have the responsibility of finding out who this is. And what happened to her? I expect to see you back this afternoon with some information, or I will contact the authorities."

He looked like he would argue with me, but I shook my head in disgust and turned away. I spent the next hour cleaning the wounds, rubbing anti-biotic ointment on her cuts, and bandaging them as best as possible.

Girija walked in while I was examining her arm, which was definitely fractured. I wheeled the portable X-ray machine and tried to get a picture of her injury. She was moaning as I pushed her arm to get the best angle for the X-ray.

"Sorry," I muttered, sweat forming on my forehead.

I was glad when I finished. I could see the woman had a severe break. She will need to see a surgeon. I made her as comfortable as possible with a splint.

"Oh, Dr. Sunny." Girija said worriedly, watching me finish tying the splint. "What happened to her?"

There was such pure fear in her voice that I felt compelled to go and put an arm around her.

"Girija, I could use some warm water."

"What happened to her?" she asked again.

I shook my head.

"She looks like she was beaten, but I don't know anything about her, not even her name. Go on and get me the water."

She returned a few minutes later with a metal bucket filled with warm water. I used the water to wash the girl's frail body. She looked about seventeen years old and was very thin. Her hair was long and thick, and her cotton sari was sturdy. I cut off her sari blouse to see the cuts on her neck and back.

Girija watched me.

"Who could do such a thing?" I wondered aloud.

I heard sobbing behind me. Surprised, I turned around. Girija was weeping silently. I covered my patient with a sheet and went to the crying woman.

"Girija, what is the matter?"

I led her to the waiting area and pulled her beside me on a bench.

I put my arms around her as she wept uncontrollably for a long while, and then she stopped, hiccupping a little.

"I'm sorry, Dr. Sunny," she said, wiping her face and eyes with her sari. "It's just that this has brought back a lot of bad memories."

Girija told me her story. "It happened long ago when I was a young girl. My family lived in a small village where my father was a farmer. It was a place of suffering and deprivation. We were always on the verge of starving and dependent on the rains. My family lived in a mud hut in the middle of the land we leased from the local landowner. My father grew wheat and sorghum on the land, and after the harvest, we paid our share to the landowner. But the crop was very meager this year, and my two brothers and I were always hungry. The rains never came, and the earth cracked under the hot sun. My mother went to the local temple every day to pray for rain.

"When the landowner asked for our rent, my father had nothing to give him. I was seventeen, and my brothers were a few years younger than I was. They left the farm, hoping to find work in the city. My parents had hoped to marry me off, but with no dowry, I had no suitors. The following year, the rains came, and the harvest was slightly better. My mother was able to find money to buy me a new sari, and my marriage was arranged. I met my husband-to-be on the day of the wedding. His family owned the grain mill in the next village and were wealthy compared to my parents. The first few days after the marriage were happy ones. I tried to do all the housework and cooking, but my mother-in-law wanted more. Her dissatisfaction rubbed off on my husband, who found fault with everything I did or said. He would smack me for the smallest thing, like the coffee not being hot enough, and then it became for no reason at all. One night, his parents were gone, and he beat me so viciously that the neighbors called the police. One of the policemen who came to my house was Ragu. I spent weeks in the local hospital. When I was finally healed, I took a bus back to my husband's home, but his mother refused to let me in. She said her son had no use for me and threw out my few belongings. She told me to never come back. I was sitting at the bus stop and didn't know what to do when Ragu saw me. He escorted me to my parents' home."

Girija paused for a moment and then continued, "A few days later, when I came home from the market, I found my mother and father both murdered. I ran out, yelling for help. My neighbor told me it was my husband who had committed this awful crime. There was a manhunt for him, but he was never caught. I would have tried to kill myself in my sorrow, but Ragu never left my side."

After Girija finished her tale, I squeezed her hand.

She sighed, "Now you know how important Ragu is to me. He kept me safe when no one else would. He brought me to the mission, and Mother Superior took me in. Even though my body was healed, my mind was not. The sisters helped to heal my mind and soul. When Ragu retired from the police force, he returned and asked me to marry him. That was just six months ago, and I have never been happier."

"Oh, Girija, I'm sorry you have suffered so much. However, I'm so happy life has become better for you."

"Oh yes, Dr. Sunny, I feel like a new woman."

"Was your husband ever found?" I asked.

"No. Ragu searched for him. His parents said they didn't know where he was. I was glad to be far away from him. I feel safe in Mahagiri."

"Are you feeling better now?"

When she nodded yes, I said, "I need to check on my patient."

"I'll bring you some tea," she said.

Like the British, Girija believed in the restorative power of a cup of tea.

"That would be great," I said. "I'm going to sit with the patient for a bit."

I pulled up a stool and sat down next to the still form of the injured girl. Her injuries didn't seem consistent with a beating. Not that I had seen too many beaten women, but her injuries looked different. Could this be a hit-and-run?

It was nearly mid-day when Ragu came in. I heard him talking to Girija, and I headed into the kitchen.

"I can't leave you alone for a few hours before you find trouble," he said, turning to me.

"Seeing the welfare of a patient is hardly getting in trouble," I said sharply as I entered the room.

"Dr. Sunny, I'm sorry," he said. "I didn't mean it like that. Girija was saying you want to take the girl to the mission?"

I nodded. "Yes, can you help?"

"Of course," he said. "I'll pull the jeep to the front of the clinic, and we can leave right away."

I turned to Girija and asked, "Will you be all right here by yourself? Or do you want to come with us?"

"I'm fine, Dr. Sunny," she said with a smile. She came up to me and placed a hand on my shoulder. "You go and take care of the girl. I will have a nice meal waiting."

Ragu was able to carry the unconscious girl by himself. I opened the jeep door so he could place her in the back seat. I sat beside her and held her steady as Ragu drove to the mission.

"Why are the gates closed?" I asked.

Ragu turned around before answering, "The sisters like some privacy and quiet on Sundays. However, this is an emergency, so they will help. I'll go and ask them to open the gates."

Soon, the gates swung open, and Ragu returned with Mother Superior and a novice. I exited the jeep and waited as Ragu and two of the nuns carried the girl. We walked into the hospital wing of the mission.

"I guess there are no days off for a doctor," Mother Superior said.

I smiled at her and said, "This is one case I could do without."

"What happened to her?"

"At first, I thought she had been beaten, but her injuries indicate she may have been hit by a vehicle. A group of villagers were standing over her when I found her.

"I did my best to patch her up, but I'm afraid she may have internal injuries."

The nun asked, "Why didn't you call for an ambulance and take her to the hospital?"

"I'm still waiting for my telephone connection, and there was no cell phone reception," I replied. "In any case, the girl woke up briefly and said she didn't want to go to the hospital. I thought you would be the best alternative for now."

The nun sighed and said, "You did the right thing, Dr. Sunny. We'll keep an eye on her, and if she doesn't take in some liquids soon, I'll have an I-V put in."

I provided some instructions to her staff.

"She will need to see a surgeon for the broken arm. It needs to be re-set before it can be plastered," I said.

"I will convince her to go to the hospital tomorrow," the nun assured me.

I knew the nuns would take good care of the girl.

We came home to a mid-afternoon meal of vegetable cutlets with ketchup, spiced nuts, and a delicate green salad made of wild greens.

CHAPTER SIXTEEN

MONDAY BLUES

Monday morning started off with a bang, a literal one. I woke up to the sound of someone knocking very loudly on the clinic's front door. I glanced at the clock; it was just past 6 a.m. I could hear Ragu opening the door and the murmur of voices. I pulled on pants, a sweatshirt, and my walking shoes. I entered the exam room to see Ragu carrying what looked like a bundle of clothing. When he placed the bundle on the exam room table, I saw it was a small child covered in blood.

Oh no. I had not yet recovered from my Sunday patient, and already, my week was starting off with another brutal injury.

I slipped on my white medical coat and hurried to the patient. A woman was standing behind Ragu, weeping and wringing her hands.

"Are you the mother?" I asked her. She just nodded.

"Alright," I said to her. "I'm Dr. Sunny. Ragu, please take her into the waiting room."

I peeled back the blanket and saw a small boy whose back had been ravaged by deep gashes. I searched for a pulse but couldn't find one. For the next few minutes, I tried everything to resuscitate the young boy. However, it was soon clear the boy was dead.

I looked at my watch: time of death: 6:33 a.m.

I felt helpless and wanted to weep, but I knew I didn't have that luxury. The woman was sitting in a chair. Her huge eyes were filled with sorrow.

I wiped my hands and approached her.

"I'm sorry, sister," I said. "The wounds were too deep, and there was too much blood loss."

She had the calm look of someone who was going to have a breakdown soon.

She nodded and whispered, "I knew he was gone."

"What happened?" I asked.

"We were collecting firewood to start our morning fire," she said, looking down at the boy. "It was dark and foggy. We went down a path to gather some twigs. It was a narrow path on the hillside, and suddenly, out of nowhere, a large jungle cat jumped out of the bushes. I was frozen with fear. My little Chittu screamed and ran. The animal chased and pounced on him like he was a tiny mouse. I threw my basket at the creature and screamed as it shook my baby. Suddenly, I heard the sound of a car. This startled the animal, and it dropped my boy and ran up the hill. I was running to my son when I heard a loud bang. Chittu was so limp and still. I knew the worst had happened."

She began to sob in anguish. I rubbed her back, feeling helpless. Ragu walked in and touched my arm.

"Dr. Sunny, can I talk to you in private?"

I followed him into the waiting room.

"What is it, Ragu?"

"Dr. Sunny," he said hesitantly, "A man drove the lady and her boy here. His jeep is parked outside. I think he's down at the tea house."

The tea house was a small stall located right beside the bus stop. The owner, Shivaji, held court from behind two steaming brass vessels. He made endless cups of tea while his wife, Yamuna, prepared simple snacks. Boiled peanuts, deep-fried noodles, and lentil cakes were on the menu. Ari had told me; Yamuna's snacks were delicious. My mother had been so adamant in her opposition to tea stall snacks that I had never developed a taste for salty, oily foods.

Besides, rumor had it that the tea stall became a toddy stall at night, especially on days the laborers were paid. I had heard that Shivaji also served cheap whiskey and beer along with the fermented palm drink.

Now, I walked outside with Ragu. It was a grey and gloomy day. The sun was trying its best to break through the heavy fog.

"Look at the front fender," Ragu said, pointing to the dent.

"Is that blood?" I asked, bending down to look closer at the stains and dents on the bumper.

It was a shiny new Toyota Land Cruiser, and the dented fender seemed out of place.

"What the hell are you doing?" an angry voice yelled. I slowly got up.

"Hey there, take it easy," Ragu said, stepping up to stand in front of me.

I pushed him aside to look at this individual. He was tall and lean and dressed in expensive-looking athletic clothes. He had a thin mustache and wore a stylish beret on his head. There was a thick gold chain around his neck and a signet ring with a sparkling white stone on his pinky finger. He looked at me and then at Ragu.

"Ah, you must be the new village doctor everyone is talking about. I'm Dorai Raj," he said, putting his right hand out, ready to shake mine.

I wasn't sure I wanted to touch him, but to keep the peace, I quickly shook his hand. I suppressed an urge to wipe my hand.

"Yes, I'm the new doctor here," I said.

"Dr. Sunny," Ragu spoke up.

"Yes," Dorai Raj said with a pleasant smile. "I'm the one who drove the poor kid here. He looked like a goner, but the mother insisted on bringing him here."

"She said she heard gunfire?" Ragu said.

"I shot the jaguar," he said. "I had heard reports that a big cat was in the area." He stared at me while he spoke, "I'm the largest landowner and like to know what's going on in my village."

His village? His arrogance was galling.

"I was just looking at your jeep," I told him. "How did you damage it?"

"Oh, that? Probably hit a deer or something."

"Hmm," I said, looking at the fender. "This doesn't look like deer fur to me."

I held up a piece of red-colored cloth I had pulled out of the car's front grille.

"Haven't we seen this type of cloth, Ragu?"

I continued. "You see, I treated a girl yesterday for such severe injuries I thought she had been beaten. I don't think that's what happened. She was run over by a car, perhaps even this car. I'm sure the hospital doctor will find evidence to prove this."

"You must be mistaken," Dorai Raj said, stammering slightly. His earlier bravado was obviously shaken.

"When the girl wakes up, she will be able to tell the police exactly what happened," Ragu said. "The forensic team will investigate. I know how these things work since I was a policeman."

All the bluster seemed to go out of Dorai Raj, and he slumped against his SUV.

"How is the girl?" he finally asked.

"She's being looked after," I said. "You don't need to know anything more."

"She must be at the mission," Dorai Raj said, standing straight. "I will talk to the Mother Superior whom I know well."

"Wait," I said.

I ran inside and came back with my cell phone. There was no cell connection, but I could still take photos with it. Dorai Raj said nothing as I took several pictures of him and the front of his car.

He left, mumbling something about making things right. What an unpleasant man. I felt like I needed to take a bath.

Inside the clinic, Girija had wrapped the child's body in an old blanket. The mother was seated in the waiting room, crying softly.

"Come," Ragu's voice was gentle. "Let's take you and the boy home."

The woman got up and turned to look at me. I went up to her and drew her into my arms.

"I'm sorry about your beautiful son. When you are ready, come and tell me some stories about him."

I watched Ragu pick up the body and lead the mother out the door.

"Dr. Sunny," Girija called. "Come and have some breakfast before you open the clinic."

I wasn't hungry, but the oat porridge with nuts and fruit was tasty, and I ate a few bites.

"This is tasty," I said. "What is it?"

"It is a locally grown grain cooked in milk and sweetened with Sister Clarice's honey."

After several cups of tea, I felt more energetic. I really wished I could talk to my mother.

"Dr. Sunny," Girija came in. "The telephone company has sent a man to set up the phone and computer."

I went to the living room to meet the man and tell him what I wanted. He said it would take a couple of hours. I opened the clinic, concentrated on the patients, and forgot about everything else.

A few hours later, Girija interrupted me with a restorative cup of tea. I wandered outside and saw Ganesha and Lingam digging in the front yard.

Around lunchtime, there was a lull, and I went to the living room to find a simple tomato soup, fresh bread, and a green salad waiting for me on the table.

"Has Ganesha and Lingam had lunch?" I asked Girija.

"Oh yes, they just returned from having lunch at the tea stall."

When the telephone man asked me to call on the newly installed landline, I knew who I'd call first.

"Amma?" I asked.

"No, this is Devi. Is that you, Dr. Sunny?" Devi asked.

I laughed at the sound of her familiar voice.

"Yes. I finally have a working telephone in the clinic," I said. "How is everyone? How are you?"

"I'm fine. Bindita keeps us busy," Devi said. "Ahh, here comes your Amma. I'll give the phone to her."

I knew Devi hated talking on the phone, so I wasn't hurt she hadn't bothered to ask about me.

"Thangam?" my mother's voice was like music to me. I felt tears gathering in the back of my throat.

I cleared my throat and replied, "Yes, Ma. We finally have a phone."

I spent the next few minutes telling her about recent events.

"Ma," I said. "Do you still have that old bed in the store room?"

"I think so," she said. "Why do you ask? I thought you already had a bed."

"I do, but my housekeeper and her husband need one and some basic furniture like a dresser."

I heard someone enter the waiting room.

"Ma, I have to go. A patient just walked in. Why don't you talk to my housekeeper and find out what they need? Her name is Girija."

I handed the phone to Girija, who was standing by the door. She tried to say she didn't want to talk, but I covered the mouthpiece and said, "Talk to my mother and get some furniture for your room."

She reluctantly took the receiver from me and said in a hesitant voice, "Hallo? Hallo?"

I left her and went to deal with my patient.

CHAPTER SEVENTEEN
UMA

The phone rang, a jarring sound I would have to get used to.

"Dr. Sunny, this is Mother Superior. I'd like you to come by when you have a quiet moment.

"Of course, is the girl doing alright?"

"Yes, she is awake and even managing to eat and drink. See you soon."

She hung up. I stood by the phone for a long moment, thinking. Since I had no clue what to expect, I decided not to worry about what was happening at the mission. The Mother Superior was a very sensible person.

As soon as breakfast was done and I had seen the few patients who had arrived that morning, Ragu and I set off for the mission. We drove all the way up to the open gate.

"Dr. Sunny," Ragu said. "I'll wait in the courtyard while you go and see the Mother."

A novice was in the courtyard watering the herbs; she put down the watering can and asked me to follow her. She showed me into the parlor and said, "I'll tell Mother you are here."

I sat down in the now-familiar room.

"Ah, Dr. Sunny, you are prompt," Mother Superior said as she entered. "I'm so glad to see you."

She sat down beside me on the sofa.

"Now, what I'm about to tell you may…." She stopped as a novice came in with a tray.

"Sister Clarice prepared this ginger tea with wildflower honey," she said, holding the tray before me.

I accepted a cup with a smile.

"Sister, can you please close the door when you leave?" Mother Superior asked.

The novice placed the tray on the table and left, closing the door quietly behind her.

I sipped spicy tea with ginger and tasted summer flowers. It warmed me right up.

"As I was saying," the nun said, setting her untouched tea on the table beside the sofa. "Last night, we had a visitor. A Mr. Dorai Raj came to see me."

I, too, put my cup down.

"Oh? I wanted to talk to you about that," I said. "I think his car was the one that hit the girl. What is her name?"

"Her name is Uma," the nun said. "Mr. Dorai Raj said you might say that. He explained that he thinks someone used his car without his knowledge or permission."

"I'm sure the police will get to the bottom of it," I countered.

The nun hesitated and looked down at her hands.

"Mother, you will call the police, won't you?" I asked.

"Listen, Dr. Sunny, this is an impossible situation. If the police investigate, it could take months, and nothing could come of it."

"Maybe they would find him guilty, and he would face charges," I said.

"That is a possibility, but his family is well-known here, and it may all come to nothing."

She had something on her mind.

"What are you proposing, Mother?"

"This may not sound good to you, Dr. Sunny, but the man has arranged to take care of Uma and all her expenses. He will also establish a fund for her family."

"He bought his way out of criminal charges?" I asked in a stern voice.

I was furious and disappointed in the nun.

"I know this sounds callous, but we have to be practical and realistic," she said. "The girl will heal and have some money for a dowry. Her family will have some money to get through the winter. In an ideal world, he would go to prison and pay for his...."

I rudely interrupted her, "Mother, this is not justice. This is a travesty."

"Dr. Sunny," her voice was sharp. "Please don't be impertinent. I didn't make this decision in haste. I thought about Uma and her family. They are the victims here, and my responsibility is to her. I won't be lectured by a girl."

I was shocked by her vehemence and sentiment. I stood up.

"Mother Superior, thank you for telling me," I said shortly. "I have to get back to the clinic."

I didn't wait for her reply and left the room. I walked through the courtyard to where Ragu was waiting for me.

"Ragu," I said. "I need a walk by myself. I'll walk back to the clinic."

"It's a long way," he said. "Are you sure?"

"I am. I need to clear my head; the walk will help me do that. You can come looking for me if I don't show up in a couple of hours."

He wasn't happy to leave me, but I gave him no choice.

The sun was warm on my back as I started up the hill. Strong women were a blessing and curse in my life. My mother ruled her home and kitchen with an iron-clad hand and a deceptive, gentle touch. We never knew when we were being manipulated. I loved her unconditionally but wasn't blind to her faults either. As Little Mother, she was the guardian/mother of the entire community, and that meant Appu and I were sometimes neglected. Meena had taken my mother's place in many ways. She was kind and gentle with us, especially after our father died. I remember how needy Appu and I had been, never leaving her side. But as Meena grew up, she became increasingly like my mother. She was independent and strong-willed and wasn't afraid of anything. She found a way to go to California and married a man who shared her passion. I didn't begrudge my sister her happiness or love, but I had felt abandoned and alone when Meena left, and Appu and I were sent to boarding school.

That desolate feeling of being completely alone and helpless was awful, and now it all came rushing back. I felt angry tears flowing down my cheeks, and I wiped them roughly off my face. I wasn't weak or helpless. I knew I was right. People couldn't go around hurting others and getting away with it. I always had an exaggerated sense of right and wrong.

I looked down at all the villages, just tiny dots among the green tea estates. High on the hill was Dorai Raj's place. Mother Superior had said the money he gave Uma would help her and her family. If Uma and her family were ready to forgive Dorai Raj, who was I to say they shouldn't? It was not my place to judge them. You can't afford to take the high ground when you are poor. I wondered who had said that. Probably my mother. I smiled to myself, got up, and started walking toward home. Yes, home. All these tiny villages filled with people were now my responsibility. I vowed to take care of them as best as I could. And I would ask Mother Superior for her help. If her conscience was clear, then I knew mine could be too.

CHAPTER EIGHTEEN
A SURPRISE VISITOR

My legs were tired from the long hike. As I neared the clinic, I saw a large lorry parked on the street. Oh, no, what tragedy awaited me now? I had visions of accidents and bloody bodies as I picked up the pace.

Girija saw me and rushed up to me. "Dr. Sunny, you have a big surprise waiting for you."

"What's going on?"

"You'll see," she said with a mysterious smile.

I walked up the steps to the clinic, thinking I had a patient, but Girija stopped me and directed me to my living quarters.

The living room had been transformed with a thick carpet and a large armchair. There was also a table lamp and a standing lamp. I looked around at the now-cozy space.

"Thangam," a voice called out from the kitchen area. I knew that voice.

"Amma!"

"In person," she came toward me with arms outstretched. We hugged, and I could feel emotion clogging my throat. We pulled away at the same time.

"Let me look at you, *kutty*," she said. "It seems like you've matured."

"Ma, it has only been a few weeks," I said. "Anyway, what are you doing here?"

"After your phone call, I decided to scrounge around the storeroom, and then Meena and Raj got involved. Turns out Mac had a few things stored in his old place."

Mac, the Scotsman, had settled in Mahagiri many decades ago and was a good friend to all of us.

"Come see what we've done with Girija's bedroom."

The plain room with a pile of blankets was also given a face-lift. There was a large iron bed with a thick mattress piled high with pillows and blankets. A chest of drawers with a mirror and another large cupboard were flush against the wall. There was a cheery red and green rug on the floor.

"So that's what the lorry is doing in front of the clinic," I said. "This looks amazing."

I looked around for Girija, who was standing by the open doorway.

"Are you happy, Girija?"

"I'm so grateful," she said. "This is now my home in every sense."

"Little Mother," she addressed my mother. "I've prepared a meal."

"Amma, you should taste her food. It's amazing," I said. "Every day, she makes something new and delicious."

"I'm surprised you taste the food," my mother said teasingly.

I was not known for my discerning palate.

"Doctoring gives me an appetite," I said with a laugh. "Talking about doctoring, I better check there are no patients in the waiting room."

I started to go toward the clinic and stopped as a thought occurred to me, "Amma, who drove the lorry?"

"Look behind you," she said.

Our cowhand, land manager, and a faithful family friend, Bhojan, stood by the clinic door. His smiling face was a familiar and welcome sight.

"Bhoja," I greeted him as I hugged him. "Thank you for bringing Amma and all these amazing things."

"Dr. Sunny," he said. "I'm happy to help."

We left the clinic door open while everyone sat at the dining table for a meal. My mother insisted that Bhojan and Ragu join us.

"What's going on here?" a voice asked from the open doorway. It was Ari.

He, too, was asked to join us.

Girija lived up to my hype and had prepared a fantastic meal. Baby carrots were seasoned with delicate dill leaves, and potatoes were baked in hot coals topped with golden ghee and a spicy seasoning mix. There was a dal soup thick with red spinach and coconut milk and plenty of hot, flaky flatbreads. The late lunch was followed by cups of tea and sweet, cardamom-spiked chickpea bars. There were also bananas and grapes.

"If I eat like this daily, I'll be as big as a house," my mother said. "Everything was delicious and amazing, Girija. And more than anything else, I could taste the love in every dish. You are doing a wonderful job of taking care of my baby."

"Amma," I said. "At 28, I'm hardly a baby."

"You'll always be a *kutty to* us," Bhojan said.

"Amma, come and see the clinic."

Since her last visit, I have upgraded my waiting room and examination area. There was my new landline and computer station.

"Everything looks great," she said, turning to me. "Have I told you how proud I am of you?" she asked, her voice thick with emotion.

She stopped me from speaking with a hand gesture.

"They say the evidence of good parenting is sometimes so far in the future that it is not always appreciated. But I'm so fortunate to see how my children have turned out. A parent is only as good as his or her child, and I'm so lucky."

I felt tears welling up.

"Oh, Ma," I said. "Meena, Appu, and I are the lucky ones. You showed us the way, and we just followed. We didn't have to do anything."

We hugged and held tightly onto each other.

"Little Mother," Bhojan said, coming into the room. "We should leave before it gets too late. I can't drive this big lorry in the dark."

Girija followed my mother to the vehicle. "Little Mother, you should come back soon. The village will be having a formal opening for the clinic."

I looked at Girija and asked, "What? What opening? How come I don't know anything about this?"

Ragu smiled, "Because you would object," he said. "It won't interfere with your patients. Mother Superior wants to see the place, and we will invite a few headmen and women from the neighboring villages."

"There's really nothing to see," I protested.

"Don't worry about it, Dr. Sunny," Ragu said. "It's all been taken care of."

I had no idea what he was talking about and wasn't sure I liked what they had planned. But I didn't want to dampen their enthusiasm. Why did I feel as if I was no longer in charge here?

CHAPTER NINETEEN
SUNSHINE CLINIC

D uring the next few weeks, Ragu, Mother Superior, and even my family conspired against me in the nicest possible way.

It all started early Friday morning when I was called to attend a breech birth. Ari offered to drive me to the village. When we arrived, the local midwife had delivered a healthy baby. I checked the vital signs of both the mother and baby and found them to be healthy. I then asked Ari to take me back to the clinic, but the family was convinced my presence was the reason for the auspicious birth of a boy.

I was asked to sit in the only chair and was served coffee with so much jaggery sugar that it hurt my teeth to sip on the hot liquid. Then, it was time for ragi balls floating in a thick vegetable chili sauce. I gamely finished two balls and refused a second helping.

Then, it was time for the celebration. Little boys and men danced. A girl sang a song from a popular film. I clapped and cheered them on. I glanced at my watch; I had been here for over three hours. Time to get back to the clinic. I congratulated the young woman and her family and, after a lengthy goodbye, left the village.

It was past midday when we returned. Ari drove me to his house instead of the clinic.

"Why are we going to your house?" I asked him.

"Dr. Sunny, Nandi would like to speak with you."

If Nandi needed advice, of course, I wanted to see her. I just wished she would have come to the clinic, like every other patient.

I walked to the headman's house and found Nandi waiting with the compulsory cup of hot tea.

I accepted the beverage and placed my bag on the table.

"What seems to be the trouble? Are you not feeling well?"

"Oh, no, Dr. Sunny," she said, sitting on the bench across from me. "I just wanted a quick word with you before you head to the clinic."

"Alright," I said, a little puzzled. "Have you noticed patients waiting at the clinic? I've been gone a long time."

"How was the birth?" she asked instead.

"It went well. It was a healthy baby boy," I said a little impatiently.

"There are rumors that Dorai Raj is in ill-health," Nandi said, leaning toward me.

Dorai Raj was the largest landowner in the area. I knew he was behind the hit-and-run, and even though he had paid off the victim, I wasn't happy about the whole situation.

"Really? Where did you hear that?"

"Oh, just talk from other villagers, but I thought you should know," she said.

I stood up. "Thank you for telling me. Is there anything else?"

Nandi paused and looked at the clock on the wall before replying, "No, I'll walk with you to the clinic."

As we walked the short distance, I couldn't help noticing there were no villagers milling about.

"Where is everyone?"

Usually, there was a group of men and women by the colossal tree, waiting for the bus or gossiping in the sun.

"I guess everyone is busy," she replied in a vague tone.

As we approached the clinic and house from the back, I hoped no patients were waiting for me.

Nandi hurried ahead and opened the back door.

"Surprise!" several voices yelled from inside the house.

I walked through the kitchen to find the living room crowded with people. More people were gathered in the clinic's waiting room.

I looked around at the crowd.

"What is going on?" I asked in a bewildered tone.

"It is the clinic's grand opening," Ari said, walking up to the front of the crowd. "Many people have come to celebrate."

"I can see that," I said.

Then, I noticed familiar faces.

"Amma? Meena? Raj?"

I was scooped up in a family hug. Bindita wrapped her arms around me.

"Bindita, you've grown so much since I last saw you," I told my niece.

"I'm here for a party," she said solemnly.

"Party? I hadn't heard about any party," I said, pretending to pinch her nose. "If it's a party, where's the cake, smarty pants."

"Cake is here," Meena said.

I stood and saw a humongous cake with the words *Best Wishes to the new Sunshine Clinic.*

I remembered when Sister Clarice had thought up a name for the clinic and hadn't given it much thought since then.

"Is that what this building is now called?" I asked.

My mother said, "We thought it was a clever take on your name."

"I helped choose this auspicious name," Bhadra said, pushing her way to the front of the crowd. "The stars say this name will bring good fortune to the village."

Since Bhadra was involved, I knew I had no choice. The villagers thought of her as a goddess-incarnate, and she had the final say in all village affairs.

"Come, it's time to cut the ribbon," Ari said, herding me outside. That's when I noticed a bright red ribbon strung around the clinic entrance. I was given a large pair of scissors to cut the ribbon. Everyone cheered.

Villagers came up to congratulate me and formally welcomed me to the village. I was amazed at the number of people who had turned up.

"Mother Superior," I breathed. "You're here!"

"Of course, child. This is an important day for the clinic. Girija showed me all the improvements, and the place looks amazing. You are already putting your stamp on the place."

"What do you think of the name?" I asked.

"It's a wonderful name. The villagers have claimed this place as their own and have approved the name. You must be immensely proud."

Everyone helped themselves to the cake, fried lentil cakes, hot tea, and bananas. I sat on the sofa surrounded by my family.

"This is an amazing place," Raj said. "And obviously, the villagers are fond of you."

I laughed and replied. "You have no idea."

"Life is not a straight line, *kutty*," my mother said.

Meena rolled her eyes, "Here comes Ma's wisdom."

Raj nudged Meena, "Come on, you are the first to follow her advice."

My mother ignored their banter and continued, "Life is like a river. It flows on, regardless of what we think or want. There are deep currents and warm shallow pools, but the forward movement is relentless. Your life in this village is like that flowing river with all the ups and downs."

I nodded, tears filling my eyes when I thought of the little boy who had been mauled by the big cat.

"And a doctor's life is especially filled with heartbreak and joy," my mother said, noticing my tears. "But didn't you just deliver a healthy baby boy today?"

I had to laugh. "It was a big scheme to get me out of the clinic for the day. The midwife was more than capable of managing the birth. I should have known something was going on because there were too many songs, dances, and cups of awfully sweet tea."

Meena and Raj laughed, and my mother smiled.

"You always hated sugar in your tea," Meena said. "Girija was just telling me you have trained the tea stall owner at the market to make your order sugar-free."

I smiled. "You wouldn't believe how much sugar these people put in their drinks."

When everyone had finally left, I helped Girija and Ragu clean up. It had been a wonderful day. I walked outside and looked up at the brand-new sign: *Sunshine Clinic* and the large yellow sun smiling down on me.

Yes, the name had a certain ring to it.

CHAPTER TWENTY

DORAI RAJ

Several months after the official opening of *Sunshine Clinic*, I received a call from Mother Superior.

"Dr. Sunny, Can you come over later this week? I need to consult you on something."

I was quiet for a moment. I hadn't forgotten how the nun had taken Dorai Raj's side, even though I knew and understood why she had done it. Seeing her at the opening ceremony had lessened the tension between us; however, my reply was a little stiff.

"Of course, Mother Superior," I said. "When would you like me to come?"

"Can you make it on Sunday? It will also allow us to catch up on some things."

I agreed to visit her on Sunday. I wondered about her request, but my thoughts were interrupted by an emergency at the clinic. Two families from different villages had an ongoing feud, and the result was two young men were injured. I stitched them up as best as possible and sent them to the government hospital for X-rays.

After a breakfast of porridge and apples on Sunday morning, I set off on foot to the mission using a shortcut. Ragu agreed to come pick me up in a few hours.

"I'll call you," I told him. "Then you won't need to wait."

Ragu had been fixing things in the clinic. I knew he liked working on Sundays when the clinic was closed.

It was a beautiful, warm day. I stopped at the top of a small hill and looked over the green and lush valley. I couldn't imagine living anywhere else. In the few months I had returned, this once again had become home in every sense.

I walked at a quick pace and arrived at the mission, relaxed and warm. I was starting to think the nun had the best interests of the villagers at heart, after all. Besides, she had lived here far longer than I and knew how to deal best with sensitive topics.

A novice saw me and quickly opened the gates.

"Come in, Dr. Sunny. Mother is expecting you."

I followed her down the now familiar path to the visitor's parlor. She showed me in, and I took a seat on the sofa. The Mother Superior entered a few minutes later.

"I'm sorry I kept you waiting," she said as she sat down. "There is a bit of a crisis, and I need your help."

"Of course," I replied, sitting slightly forward in my seat. "What can I do to help?"

The nun smiled. "I respect your kindness toward me, Dr. Sunny. I know I disappointed you over my decision about Uma and Dorai Raj."

I was about to say something, but she held up her hand.

"Please, let me speak. I apologize for what you thought was my callous disregard for the law. I have known Dorai Raj for a long time, several decades, actually. He is an ambitious man, and sometimes he makes some questionable choices."

She continued. "That is no excuse, I agree, but I want you to understand what I was trying to do. I heard Uma has recovered, and her marriage to a young man has been formalized. The family has moved into a larger home and is doing well.

"Now, my dilemma for the day."

She stood up.

"Dr. Sunny, please come with me."

A little puzzled at her mysterious behavior, I followed her out of the room and down the corridor, deep into the nuns' living quarters. This was obviously a very private part of the nunnery. The floor beneath my feet was shiny and polished. The walls were bare, save an occasional simple wooden cross. Most of the doors were closed. I assumed they were the nuns' private rooms.

Mother Superior pushed open a wooden door, and I followed her inside. The room was plainly decorated and contained a single bed which was occupied. The white walls were decorated with a cross and an artist's rendering of Mother Mary. The only furniture was a simple wooden rocking chair and a chest of drawers. There was a closed door leading to a bathroom or closet. I looked down at the person on the bed. It was Dorai Raj. All his self-confidence and swagger were gone. He was a sick, frail old man. I turned with a questioning look, and Mother Superior indicated we both kneel beside the man's bed.

"Dorai Raj has been ill for some time, but now he is dying from the final stages of pancreatic cancer," she said. "He wanted to speak with you. Can you listen to him, Dr. Sunny?"

I looked at the emancipated man. Death has a way of making everything else seem inconsequential.

"Yes, of course, Mother," I whispered.

I took the man's thin hand in mine. His bony fingers were brittle as a baby bird. He opened his eyes at my touch. It took a moment for him to recognize me.

"Dorai Raj," I said. "Can I do anything to make you more comfortable?"

"Ah, Dr. Sunny, comfort is beyond my reach now," he said weakly. "I wanted to ask for your forgiveness."

I shook my head and said, "What is past is past."

"You must think I'm an evil man. I want to tell you a story."

"You sound so tired, Dorai Raj. Please rest," I urged him. "There is no need for stories."

He ignored me, and with a faraway look, he began to talk, "Long ago, I married a beautiful girl. We were so happy until she died in childbirth, right here in the mission. The boy was a handsome and strong on the outside, but something was missing inside. For years, he lived in an institution, but in my arrogance and foolish pride, I brought him to my house thinking I could mold him into the son I had always wanted."

He paused and started to wheeze and cough. Mother Superior handed me a tumbler of water with a paper straw. Both of us helped the sick man take a sip. He lay back down, his forehead dotted with perspiration.

Dorai Raj continued in a weak voice, "For a while, things seemed to be going well. One morning, I woke up and the jeep was gone. He wasn't supposed to drive the vehicle. We found the jeep in a ditch a few miles from our house. The fender was bent and stained with blood. I thought he had hit an animal. He was found much later that day in the forest, walking in a daze. He had no recollection of the accident and couldn't tell me anything about whom or what he had hit.

"A few days later, I drove the injured boy to your clinic, and when you and Ragu pointed out the bent fender, I couldn't believe my son had hit a woman. But in the deepest part of my heart, I knew it was probably true. With the Mother Superior's help, I've placed him back in an institution. He will no longer be a danger to anyone else. He will be looked after for the rest of his life."

The man grasped my hand and raised his head off the pillow to look into my eyes.

"I want you to know that if he had the mental capacity, I would have turned him in to the police to be punished."

He paused to take a breath.

I spoke now, wanting him to understand my sentiments.

"Dorai Raj, you are a father and wanted to protect your son. You acted with the best intentions. I can see that now."

Tears ran down his face, slipping into the deep grooves of his cheeks.

"I just wanted you to know I'm sorry," he said, sobbing.

I felt tears gathering in my eyes, and I squeezed his hand and whispered, "I understand. You can be at peace now."

I held his hand until his breathing slowed, and he fell into a deep sleep.

A touch on my shoulder startled me. I had forgotten Mother Superior was next to me.

"Dr. Sunny, come, let him rest," she said.

I got up feeling stiff and followed her out. We walked down the long corridor and into the visitor's parlor. The room seemed warm and cheery after the one I had just left. I sank into the sofa.

"Life is complicated," I said. "Cancer is not a pretty disease."

Mother Superior nodded and said, "No, it is not. Life is indeed complicated, dear one. Those are wise words. As a woman of God, I wrestle with that dilemma every day. Life is not in black and white or even grey. It is a myriad of colors and experiences. Humans can make everything wonderful, complicated, and hopeless simultaneously."

"I'm sorry I was so hasty in judging you," I said. "I have a lot to learn."

She smiled and replied, "We all do. I may be older, but it's never too late to keep learning. Today, you taught me something."

"What?" I asked in surprise.

"How to forgive graciously and accept an apology. Because of your kindness, a sad, lonely man will die in peace. Ultimately, we all have to face our Creator with a clear heart and conscience."

CHAPTER TWENTY-ONE

BHADRA

"Bhadra, come in and sit down," I said, gesturing to a chair. "How are you?"

She shook her head. "I'm not sure, Dr. Sunny. I feel fine, but there are some bad omens."

"Omens?"

"Yes, bad portents. I left out a pan of water under the full moon and this morning when I looked into the reflection I saw some inauspicious events. On my way here, I was sure I saw the one-eyed beggar who always appears when evil is abroad."

"Something is going on."

She leaned forward and pulled down her sari so that I could see the tops of her breasts.

"Here," she pushed her fingers into the fleshy part of her chest. "I feel something hard. It was smaller a few months ago."

I felt a sinking sensation in my stomach. Crying babies looked good right about now.

I examined her and felt a lump, the size of a paisa coin, in her right breast.

"Alright, Bhadra, you can get dressed," I said.

We sat in the corner of the exam room which now had a small table, a tiny sofa, and a couple of chairs. My mother and Girija had made this tiny space feel cozy and safe.

"Bhadra, I will call the hospital today and make an appointment with the lab. You need to get a mammogram, a sort of photo of the inside of your breast," I said.

"Then what happens?"

"Well, depending on what we see, we can figure out a course of treatment."

"Is this cancer?" She sound frightened.

I wished I could comfort her. This was a dreaded question. No one liked to hear this diagnosis.

"I can't say for sure until we do further tests," I said. "Let's wait for the results."

"I just want to know what's going on," she said, despairing.

I placed my hand over hers and said, "I know the waiting can be the hardest part."

She looked me in the eye.

"I don't have the strength for this," she said.

"If anything, I'd say you are the strongest person in the village," I replied. "I've heard your story. You can handle anyone or anything and certainly a small lump."

She laughed a dry chuckle between a sob and giggle and said, "I suppose so. Did you hear the story of the cowherder?"

I shook my head.

"I was young then and a bit foolhardy. The women didn't want to go to a male doctor, especially for sensitive problems. A young mother brought me her little girl. She was a sweet thing, barely six years old. Someone had lured her with a piece of candy and then brutally assaulted her. Can you imagine someone doing that to a child? I took care of the little one's physical pain.

I prayed for her soul and mind. Eventually, she healed, but I became the avenging Goddess Kali. I persuaded the mother to tell me the name of the attacker."

She sighed and continued. "It was a local cow herder. He lived in a shack in the hills and tended the cows that roamed the pastures. He was paid by cattle owners who appreciated his efforts to keep their animals safe. I spent a week hiding among the tea bushes, watching the man. He was an ordinary middle-aged man. Every market day, he would come down to the maidan. On this day, I watched as he bought a bag of sweets and wandered around the marketplace. I followed him as he watched the kids play on the grass. He found a small girl sitting by herself, watching everyone else play. He offered her a sweet, but the smart girl refused. He shrugged and ate a sweet. The girl watched him, and when he offered her some candy again, she took it. He shared more sweets and then whispered something in her ear. Obediently, she got up, took his hand, and they started walking away from the crowd. The man looked around nervously but no one was paying any attention to him."

"Except you," I said.

She nodded before continuing. "The power of the Goddess was strong within me that day as I followed the pair. He led her into a secluded area behind the cattle pen. I found him on top of the terrified girl. With a terrible screech, I strode over and straddled him, grabbed him by his greasy hair. I was about to cut his throat with the sharp tea-cutting knife when I happened to glance down at the young child's terrified eyes. I roared again, and people at the market said it sounded like thunder rolling out of the hills. Some of the villagers ran to investigate and pulled me off the man. I won't go into all the details, but the Goddess's blood thirst was slaked that evening. The body of the herder was never found, and the entire village took an informal vow of silence when the police came to investigate."

Bhadra paused for a long moment and said, "It was that incident that made me take on a life of celibacy and goddess worship. I vowed to be the guardian of the village women and children."

I squeezed her shoulder.

She got up wearily. "I'll be on the morning bus to the hospital," she said on her way out.

At lunch, I asked Girija, "Who would I contact to find support for Bhadra?"

"What's wrong with her?"

I shook my head as I chewed the wholegrain tomato sandwich I was eating for lunch.

"I can't give out any details, but she will need the help of the villagers in the coming months."

"What do you need me to do?"

"Tomorrow, she is going to the government hospital for some tests, and it would be nice if the villagers could show her some support. She is taking the first bus to Lower Mahagiri."

"I'll take care of it, Dr. Sunny," Girija said, a thoughtful look on her face.

The following day, Girija knocked on my bedroom door.

"Dr. Sunny, you need to come see this."

It was barely 5 a.m., I quickly slipped on pants and a sweatshirt and went outside. I blinked at seeing a massive crowd of mostly women in front of the clinic. I looked over the heads of the gathered women and saw another, even larger group by the bus stand.

"What is going on, Girija?"

"You asked for support," she said with a smug smile. "They are here to show their concern and love for Bhadra."

I stood in the open doorway and sipped hot coffee. I watched Bhadra stop in confusion as she approached the bus stop. One of the women ran up to her, and I could see her excited hand gestures. Bhadra shook her head in amazement and then glanced over at me.

I raised my coffee cup to Bhadra, who yelled, "Dr. Sunny, do you see how many women have come to see me off? This is a good omen."

The women hugged and patted Bhadra's shoulder and back as she passed. Many were weeping. Ari and Nandi drove up in his jeep and gestured for Bhadra to get in. The crowd cheered as she drove off.

"I wish all my mornings started with a cheering crowd," I told Girija.

CHAPTER TWENTY-TWO
THE SCOTTISH PATIENT

O n Sunday mornings, I liked to take long hikes. Villagers were getting used to my eccentric ways. Summer
was ending, but the day was still warm. Today, I was
the only one on the path, and when I reached the top of a hill,
I paused to take in the breathtaking view. I could make out the
jacaranda tree in front of Ari's house and the cluster of white-
washed houses on the distant hillside. If I squinted I could almost see Girija in the garden with the three small hens beside
her. She locked them up at night in a coop Ragu had built next
to the outhouse.

A sudden movement to my immediate right caught my eye.
What was it? Was it an animal? I walked cautiously down the hill
and found a man lying on the path. I knelt down and did what
was natural to me. I checked his pulse, which was rapid but fairly
strong. He was lying on his side, so I rolled him onto his back.
He was a foreigner with reddish brown hair and tanned skin.
His face was red and flushed and his forehead was warm to my
touch. He probably had a fever. How did a foreigner end up on
this path in the middle of a tea estate? I unbuttoned his shirt and
saw no wounds on his chest. His belly was soft. His breathing
was steady. I raised his eyelids to look at his pupils, which were

dilated. I removed my jacket, rolled it up, and placed it under his head. Luckily, his head was in the sparse shade of a tea bush. I wondered how long he had been lying here.

I patted him lightly on the cheeks.

"Wake up, wake up. Can you hear me?"

There was no response.

He was wearing shorts and sneakers. I sat back and looked at the prone man. I turned over his left arm and saw it had a deep gash on it. The wound was definitely infected; I could see angry red marks streaking up his arm. He needed help right away. I pulled out my cell phone, not expecting to see a signal. I was amazed to see three whole bars. I hadn't seen such a strong signal since I left home a few months ago.

"You are fortunate," I said to the unconscious man.

I dialed the clinic, and Ragu picked it up after the second ring.

"Sunshine Clinic," he answered.

"Ragu," I replied. "It's me."

"Dr. Sunny, where are you calling from? I thought you were hiking."

"I was hiking, Ragu, but now I have a medical problem."

"Are you alright?" he asked in a concerned voice. "Are you hurt?"

"I'm fine, Ragu. I'm on the hill opposite our clinic. I found an unconscious man lying on the path. He has a fever and is not responding. I need your help to get him to the clinic."

"Of course," he said. "Let me see, how will I find you? Are you by any road?"

"No, but judging by the sun, I'm west, just below Dorai Raj's estate, and I can see the clinic from here," I replied. "If you come outside to the back, near the chicken coop, and look west, you may be able to see me."

I stepped off the path and stood on the edge of the hill. I took off my white T-shirt and started waving it like a flag.

"Ragu, can you see me?" I spoke into my phone.

"Dr. Sunny, this is Girija. Ragu is looking for you from the back of the house."

"Alright, Girija, put down the phone and tell Ragu look for me waving a white T-shirt like a flag. I'm standing about halfway up the hill."

"I'll be right back," she promised.

I kept waving my shirt. Finally, I could see Ragu look in my direction and wave back. He ran back into the house.

"Dr. Sunny," his voice on the phone was breathless. "I know where you are. I can come to you in the jeep. Do you need me to bring anything?"

"Yes. You can bring the medicine bag, which is by the door, and the stretcher. Can you see if Ari or someone can come with you? We will need help to get him into the jeep. I need to start an IV and get some antibiotics in him right away. How long will it take you"?

"About 30 minutes."

"Oh, so long? All right, hurry, please."

I hung up.

"Wow, am I dead and in Indian heaven?" a voice asked from behind me.

The man was awake and looking at me with blatant interest. I then realized I was wearing only my athletic bra.

I jumped down from the embankment.

"You're awake," I said a little redundantly.

"And you are not a half-dressed angel? And I'm not dead?" he said, obviously pleased with himself.

I hastily tugged on my T-shirt.

"Now, I know I'm not dead," the man murmured.

"Do you know where you are?"

"Outside?" he suggested.

"Good guess," I replied. "How about your name?"

He thought for a moment, wrinkling his forehead. I couldn't help noticing his blue eyes. They somehow looked remarkably familiar.

Callum," he said.

"Okay, Callum," I said. "That's an interesting name."

"Are you familiar with Scottish names?"

"No," I replied. "Are you Scottish?"

"Hmm," he said, closing his eyes.

"Don't go back to sleep. I need you to stay awake."

"Why?" he asked.

"Just stay with me. You can't go to sleep. Tell me what happened?"

"Why? You're not a doctor, are you?" he asked sleepily.

"Actually, I am," I said. "So, what happened to you?"

"You don't look old enough to be a qualified doctor," he countered.

I frowned at him.

He continued, "I was walking, enjoying this fine day when the world turned topsy-turvy, and that's all I remember."

I sat on my haunches next to him.

"I'm going to check the back of your head," I said, gently probing the back of his head.

There was a large knot.

"Ouch," he said as I touched a sore spot.

"Sorry, looks like you hit your head on a rock when you fell down. That's probably why you lost consciousness," I said. "It looks like you might have a concussion."

He protested. "I played rugby and never once had a concussion."

"Maybe it was the combination of fever and getting hit on the head that made you lose consciousness," I said. I sat back on my heels and looked at him. He met my stare.

"What's the plan, doc?"

I replied, "Well, I do have a plan. Help is on the way."

In fact, I could hear the sound of the jeep in the distance. I stood up and looked up at the path.

"Are you going to take off your t-shirt and wave again?" he asked with a smile.

I blushed.

I was about to reply when I saw the jeep about thirty yards above us. It came to a stop in a cloud of dust. Ragu got out and looked around.

"Down here," I yelled.

He clamored down the hill, fighting his way through the tea bushes.

"Dr. Sunny," he said. "I have Ari and a laborer with me."

I replied, "Let's get him up to the jeep. We can take him to the mission, which is closer than the clinic."

Ari yelled to the two men to bring the stretcher.

"Dr. Sunny," Ari said, peering at the man on the ground. "This is Scot Sir."

"You know him?" I asked Ari.

"Yes, of course. He just bought Dorai Raj's estate."

I knew Dorai Raj was dying.

"What is his name?"

"That I don't know," Ari said. "We call him Scottish Sir."

"I told you, it's Callum," a voice said from the ground.

I looked down at him, surprised to see him so alert.

With the men's help, we got Callum to the jeep. Getting the stretcher through the tea bushes was difficult, but we finally managed to reach the road. I hoped we hadn't made any possible internal injuries worse.

I sat with Callum in the back seat, his head on my lap.

"This not the sort of ambulance drive I'm used to," he mumbled.

I tried not to show how he was getting under my skin. It was hard to ignore his bright blue eyes watching my every move.

"Close your eyes and lie still," I said.

"I thought I had to stay awake," he bantered back.

"Whatever," I muttered, clenching my jaw.

He chuckled and closed his eyes. It was a bumpy drive, and I tried to cushion his head as best as possible.

Ari jumped out and knocked on the closed gates when we pulled up to the mission. A novice soon appeared with the Mother Superior right behind her.

We managed to move Callum into the mission clinic and into a bed. I prepared an IV drip.

"Young Callum," Mother Superior's voice was affectionate. "What have you been up to now?"

"Mother Superior," he said, trying to sit up.

"Now, you stay put," the nun said, turning to me, "Mr. Callum has joined our community, coming all the way from Scotland."

"He needs to lie still," I said, pushing him down and making sure the I.V. was secure. "He may have a concussion and needs to be monitored. If he doesn't improve in a few hours, he should be taken by ambulance to the government hospital."

"Alright, Dr. Sunny," the nun said. She looked at Callum and asked, "What happened to your hand?"

"I scraped it on an iron gate and was on my way to the mission to get it looked at, but somehow, I lost my footing. Luckily, this young and beautiful doctor came to my rescue."

I blushed again and said, "Well, it was lucky I came by. You might have been lying there for days."

"All's well that ends well," Mother Superior said diplomatically. "We'll take care of him, Dr. Sunny."

"Dr. Sunny? Is that your name?"

"Yes," I replied. "I have a sunny disposition, you see."

"You could have fooled me," he said with a grin. "Although, I think the name suits you."

He was a good-looking man, and I couldn't help smiling back. At the same time, Mother Superior looked on with an interested expression.

"I'm leaving him in your capable hands, Mother," I told the nun as I left the room.

"Come back soon, Doc Sunny," the patient called cheekily from his bed.

"He seems to be improving fast," I muttered to myself.

However, I was worried about him, and later that evening I returned to the mission with Ragu.

"Couldn't keep away, could you, Doc?" the patient asked. He was sitting in bed while a novice was helping him sip broth.

"How are you feeling?" I asked, looking over his chart.

His temperature was down, and he was responding to the antibiotics. He needed a tetanus shot. I mentioned it to Sister Clarice, who was in the clinic.

"You'll have to administer it, Dr. Sunny," she said. "I'm terrible with needles."

I wasn't looking forward to this. The easiest place for the shot would be in the thick buttock muscles.

"Mr. Callum, when you finish the broth, can you lie on your side and pull down your pants?"

"Ah, ah, I knew it," he said with a huge grin. "But I'm not that easy."

"You need a tetanus shot," I said a little sharply. "Or maybe it would be good for your jaw to be closed shut? A little peace and quiet would be nice?"

"Ah, just kidding, lass," he said.

After the shot, I was about to leave when he reached over and grabbed my arm.

"Come on, Doc, have pity on a guy and sit with me? Just for a couple of minutes."

I sat on a chair beside the bed and studied Callum, who looked alert. His reddish-brown hair was tousled, and he had a blond beard growth. I liked his bright blue eyes and strong chin. He could have been on the cover of one of my sister's romance novels.

"Who are you, Dr. Sunny?" he said, turning toward me.

He certainly wasn't the silent type.

"Well, I'm the village doctor," I began.

"That I already know," he said. "Tell me where you came from or did you spring from the ground like the woman in your myths."

"You mean, Sita?"

"Yes, her."

"Actually, my family lives here in Mahagiri."

"Really? What do they do? Do you have any brothers and sisters?"

"You sound like a lawyer cross-examining a witness," I said with a laugh.

"I studied law but never took the bar," he replied.

"In Scotland?"

"Aye. Did my Scottish burr give it away?"

I smiled. "Yes, and the Mother Superior mentioned you came from Scotland. Also, Ari told me you just moved into Dorai Raj's old place."

"Oh, yes, I heard he was quite the villain."

I was quiet for a long minute, remembering Dorai Raj on his deathbed.

"Everything is not as it seems sometimes."

He studied me and said, "You sound like a cryptic Indian sage."

I changed the subject. "I have an older sister, a niece, and a twin brother."

He sat up, leaning on his elbow.

"Go on. Tell me about your parents."

It was easy to talk to him, and I told him about my father's death and how my mother had ended up becoming a successful businesswoman to provide for the family.

"She sounds quite amazing."

I nodded and said, "She is. Now, it's time for you to rest and for me to return to my restful Sunday."

I got up. He reached over and took my hand.

"Thanks for saving me today, Doc. My mother would say my hard head saved me, but it was you."

I let him hold my hand for another moment before tugging it away.

"Just doing my job," I replied, walking out of the clinic.

On the way home, I thought about Callum. His easy, flirty manner was quite different from the fellow medical college students. The men worked hard and partied even harder. Some of the girls were driven, and many felt the need to blow off steam by attending parties and drinking. My mother had filled my head about how alcohol had ruined families, so I had never been tempted to drink or party. This meant I didn't know how to respond to flirting. I had been an introvert, focused on my studies.

Now, for the first time, I wish I knew how to banter and flirt. My sister Meena had no trouble with this. I had literally lived in her (and Appu's) shadow. For one thing, both of them were much taller than me. I had inherited my mother's genes for height and her darker complexion.

After my nightly bath, I looked at my face as I smoothed cream on it. It was not a beautiful face, but it wasn't unattractive either. Like my father, I had large almond-shaped eyes and thick eyelashes. Luckily, I wasn't plagued by the infamous uni-brow like many of my cousins. My body was lithe and firm since I watched what I ate and exercised, including yoga sessions. Maybe not exactly movie-star material, but I wasn't hideous either.

CHAPTER TWENTY-THREE
CALLUM (HIKING)

Dorai Raj had sold him a losing estate. Tea production was down, and nearly all the equipment was old. The house was generally in good repair, but it still needed updates. He would have to use up most of his inheritance to upgrade the property and business. Everyone back home thought he was crazy to move to India.

"You are just like your mad uncle Mac," his father had said. "He left his family and the highlands and never came back."

It was a story about his uncle Mac that had brought him to the hillside town of Mahagiri. His late uncle Mac had stayed connected with Callum and written long letters about Mahagiri. Callum had read and re-read his uncle's letters. He had no regrets about coming here.

After spending hours with his accountant, he needed a bit of fresh air to clear his head. And besides his hand was aching. He would have to go to the village doctor, no doubt a hack, to see to it. The mission might be a better idea. He had scraped his hand on a rusty nail sticking out of a board, and now the cut looked nasty and red. It also hurt like hell. Maybe he'd have a shot of some whiskey later to take off the edge.

He wanted to forget money troubles and the aching hand and go for a hike on this beautiful Sunday morning.

The walk had started off well. The fresh air felt good, and the sun was warm on his neck. He walked down the path among the tea bushes, following the trail used by the tea pickers. He was alone on the hillside except for the hawk circling high above his head. In the distance, he could hear the crows cawing on the shores of a small lake in the valley. A mountain river fed the lake where the living came to pay homage to the dead. They held wakes, wept, and fed the crows in memory of their loved ones. The lake was too far away to see even from his high perch.

He was halfway down the hill when he stumbled on a loose stone, and before he knew it, he was on the ground. He remembered nothing else.

He remembered something: a beautiful brown girl in a bra waving a white flag. She had been like a nymph. Maybe in Mahagiri, they had tea nymphs, brown and lithe with a long, thick braid.

Of course, the minute she knelt by his side; he knew she was a pretty human. He couldn't believe she was the village doctor. Why hadn't anyone told him that the village doctor was such a lovely young thing? He would have visited her a long time ago. He enjoyed lying on her lap and making her blush. Even with her dusky, mocha-colored skin, he could tell when she blushed.

As he lay on the mission clinic bed, he reviewed what he learned about her, which was not much. But there was time. He meant to get to know her. He folded his arms under his head, which he had to unfold immediately because it made the lump on the back of his head hurt. He planned to grill Sister Clarice when she came to see him. The old nun had a soft spot for him.

CHAPTER TWENTY-FOUR
SUNNY

Time flew by, and I had no time to fantasize about Callum or anyone else. Bhadra was finally home after undergoing a mastectomy. She had finished her first course of chemo and was coming to the village to recuperate. I wanted to check on her, and while I was there, I thought I'd try vaccinating some of the younger children. I closed the clinic for the day. Girija was instructed to inform patients to return tomorrow unless it was an emergency.

It was past midday, but the fog hung in the air like a grey shroud. I shivered. Ragu was driving slowly on the bumpy road.

Ragu saw me shudder and said, "Dr. Sunny, there is no need to worry about Bhadra. She is superstitious, but she always listens to reason."

I turned to him. "I know. But I'm worried about her. The procedure can't be easy, especially for someone identifying with the Goddess."

He said, "That's precisely why she will be all right. The Goddess is complete in whatever form she takes."

I hadn't thought of it like that. We finally reached Bhadra's village, and the fog was incredibly dense in this valley. I followed Ragu to an immaculately kept house on the edge of town. The front garden was filled with the last of the summer tomatoes, the green ones desperately searching for warmth. A few beans hung onto the withering vines, and the ripening peppers provided a bit of brightness. Like most houses in the village, Bhadra had a large hallway. She had converted this space into a welcoming sanctuary. The walls were covered with paintings and depictions of the various aspects of the Divine Mother. A shrine with a burning lamp was set up against a wall. There were plenty of mats, cushions, and low stools for guests. The scent of sandalwood filled the air. Bhadra lay on a mat, propped on several pillows. Quite a few women were in the room, quietly talking and chewing on betel nuts.

The women moved aside, and I sat on a low, three-legged wooden stool.

"Bhadra," I said, touching her shoulder gently. "How are you doing?"

She opened her dark eyes, and I could see the light of the lamps reflected in her eyes. She tried to sit up, but I urged her to lie back down.

"Lie still," I said. "I'm just here to see how you are doing."

"Dr. Sunny, this has been an incredible journey. I've seen Lord Yama himself."

Lord Yama, or the God of Death, was a dark and mysterious figure in Hindu myths.

I said to Bhadra, "Tell me about this journey."

"Lord Yama is the ultimate judge. He decides the fate of each creature in this world. The night after my operation, I was in terrible pain and couldn't sleep. I should have called the nurse for help, but the pain meant I was still alive. That's when I saw Lord Yama. Despite his terrifying appearance, he is a fair and just god. He told me my female power and inner strength are not based on the length of my hair, the color of my skin, or the size of my breasts. I had to live to share this powerful and uplifting message with women everywhere.

"The Lord also had an additional request."

I said nothing. As a scientist, I was skeptical of such stories of visions and gods. However, I lived in India, the land of myths and stories, and who was I to disbelieve Bhadra's story? In any case, her mission to help other women was noble.

"He said for too long, dogs had been maligned as harbingers of death. He left me a gift."

I noticed a furry body lying on the ground beside her bed.

"This is Karuta," she said, patting the creature's head.

The dog raised its head and looked at me with warm brown eyes.

I bent over and rubbed the dog's silky ears.

"Karuta, you are well-named," I said.

"He is black as night, and it's during the blackest of nights when the light is brightest," Bhadra said.

"How are you feeling now?"

"The pain is better. I know now I will live," she said simply.

I nodded. "Studies have shown animals help with healing."

Bhadra laughed. "You need an explanation for everything, don't you, Dr. Sunny? That's all right. Karuta and I will visit you at the clinic once I able to walk."

"Let me know if you need anything," I said, getting up. "I look forward to seeing you and Karuta."

"You are a dog lover?" Bhadra asked.

"Who wouldn't love this face?" I said, looking down at the dog. "I wonder what kind of dog she is."

"She is Karuta, one of a kind," Bhadra said with a smile.

I said goodbye and went outside to find the fog was lifting.

"How is she doing?" Ragu asked.

"She believes in the power of the Goddess and I think she will be fine," I said. "We better go to the center of the village and see if I can vaccinate some children while I'm here. Did you bring the candy?"

Ragu held up a plastic bag of hard candies.

As I finished examining the last patient, I noticed an older woman standing off to one side, watching me. I walked over to her.

"Periamma," I said, respectfully addressing her. "Do you need to speak to me?"

She nodded behind the end of the sari she was using to cover her lower face.

"Come sit down," I urged her.

She followed me to the table and chairs Ragu had set up. Once seated, I asked if I could listen to her heart and lungs.

"Just to see how healthy your heart is," I explained. "All I'm doing is listening with this."

I held up my stethoscope.

She nodded, so I lifted her sari and listened to her heart beating a little fast. I assumed she was a little apprehensive about coming to see me.

"Everything sounds okay," I said. "Do you have any aches or pains?"

"I need some iron pills."

"Iron? What is your complaint?"

"For many years, my husband and I have been praying to Goddess Parvathi for a child. I thought the time for me to have a child had passed, but then a miracle happened. I'm now carrying a child."

Maybe she was younger than she looked. I would have thought she had gone through menopause by now.

I asked her, "How do you know you are with a child?"

She lowered her sari and smiled at me. No, just as I thought, she was too old to bear children. I waited for her answer.

"For the past three months, I have had no blood flow and my stomach is now showing."

She lifted her sari so I could see the bulge beneath the folds around her waist.

"How old are you?"

"Old enough to know," she said defiantly. Her smile was gone, and she pulled the sari over her face.

I was now sure this was not a normal pregnancy. I just hoped it wasn't anything serious.

"I'm glad for you," I said gently. "Can I ask you to urinate in a cup and let me make it official?"

She smiled once more. I gave her a small plastic cup with a lid.

"Wait, what is your name?"

"Kaveri," she said.

I wrote down Kaveri on the cup and handed it to her.

"Take off the lid and fill the cup for me. I will send it to the lab to be tested. Can you come to the Sunshine Clinic in a day or two?"

She nodded happily. I watched her disappear behind a tea bush and return with a cup filled with yellow fluid. There could be a miracle, and everything would be alright.

It was well past lunchtime when a girl came up to me,

"Dr. Sunny, Mother Bhadra says it has been several hours since you came to see her this morning and you must be hungry by now. She wants you to have lunch with her."

I looked up at Ragu, who had started to load up the jeep.

"Sure, we both will be there."

Ragu looked uncomfortable. "Dr. Sunny, perhaps you should go by yourself. It will be a women-only affair."

He looked so nervous that I simply said, "Alright, I'll have them send you a plate."

I walked through the village, past the temple, to Bhadra's house. This time, I entered through the smoky kitchen into a large room. A group of women were already seated on the ground with banana leaves in front of them. Bhadra was reclining on a pillow. She saw me and gestured to a place next to her.

"Come, sit down, Dr. Sunny. You must be hungry after working all morning."

"Thank you for inviting me," I said. "Can I wash my hands first?"

"Of course, show the doctor the washroom, Kami," she told a young woman.

I followed her through another doorway and found the washroom. It had a sink, an indoor toilet, and a shower. It was actually nicer than my own bathroom.

After washing up, I joined the group.

I sat down on the mat. The banana leaf in front of me was filled with rice, melted ghee, thick dal, fresh tomatoes, onions, a spicy potato curry, and deep-fried wafers.

I was hungry and scooped up the rice and dal with my fingers.

The women were watching me closely, and I looked at Bhadra questioningly.

"What's wrong? Why is everyone staring at me?"

"They were all hoping you would be eating with your spoon," she said with a laugh. "We have heard stories."

I smiled at their curiosity. "I usually use those only if I can't wash my hands. I'm Indian, after all."

"I'm glad to hear that," Bhadra said. "You must remember your heritage in the coming weeks and months."

"What do you mean?"

"Nothing, just a feeling I have."

I had no idea what she was talking about, and she wouldn't say anything more.

"Fortune telling is not a precise science," was all she said.

In fact, it wasn't a science at all. I stopped myself from saying it out loud.

"Oh, could someone make a plate of food and take it to Ragu?" I asked.

A woman laughed. "Was he scared to come eat with us women?"

"Actually, he was just embarrassed," I said.

"Men are sometimes frightened to come into this female sanctuary," Bhadra said. "Of course, Kami will send some lunch for Ragu."

She asked me, "Are you done for the day?"

"Yes," I said, taking a drink of water. "This food is delicious."

"We take turns cooking," another woman said. "Today, it was Savitha's turn; she is a good cook."

I agreed as I finished the last bite of the wafer. I got up and washed my hands.

When I came back, a woman handed me a cup of tea.

"No sugar," she said shyly.

I nodded my thanks and took a sip of the hot drink.

"Mother Bhadra is in the front room and wants to talk to you privately."

I walked through a bedroom and into the front room. Bhadra was lying on the sofa. There was a tumbler of lime water next to her.

"Do you have any nausea?" I asked.

"Now you are a fortune teller?"

"Hardly, I see you drinking lime water," I replied.

She laughed. "Come sit. I didn't mean to annoy you with my prophecy. Sometimes, the Goddess puts words into my mouth, and I just repeat them."

"It was just a strange thing to say," I said.

"Did you meet a foreigner recently?"

I was taken aback, but news travels fast in the village.

"Well, yes. A Scot has moved into Dorai Raj's place."

"You were fated to meet Dr. Sunny. That is all I can say."

"Do you need any pain medication?" I asked.

"No, I'm fine."

"Then I better get back to the village," I said, standing up.

She nodded. "I'll see you soon, Dr. Sunny."

CHAPTER TWENTY-FIVE
CALLUM'S INVITATION

It was nearly three days before Mother Superior felt it was safe for Callum to leave the mission clinic.

His hand was still bandaged, and he was feeling much better. His driver, Dilip, was waiting for him at the mission gates. The Mother Superior must have called him.

"How are you feeling, Sir," Dilip asked. "All of us were very worried when we couldn't find you."

Callum sighed. "It's a long story, Dilip. A village doctor rescued me, and I'm better now. What's going on at the estate?"

"Thambi says the estate is partially operational," he replied.

Thambi was the manager, and Callum thought he was a bit of a dodgy character.

"Good, good," he said. "Let's go straight to the factory."

As they bumped along, the jeep passed a building with a massive sign on the roof. *Sunshine Clinic.*

"Stop here," he said abruptly to the driver. "Let me go check in with the doctor."

"Yes, sir," Dilip said. "I thought you were all better."

"I am. I want to thank the doctor."

Callum jumped out of the vehicle and went up the steps to the clinic's front entrance. He was about to knock when a woman came out from another door.

"Dr. Sunny is away," she said. "I can take down your name and ask her to give you a call."

He looked at the woman. "Alright. I'm Callum MacPherson from Dorai Raj's estate."

"Oh, I know who you are," the woman said. "Our Dr. Sunny rescued you."

"Well, yes." He said, a bit taken aback. "That's why I'm here, actually. I wanted to thank her in person. Do you have any idea when she'll be back?"

"She's following up on some of her patients in the village," the woman said. "But you can leave your name and number here."

She handed him a clipboard.

He scribbled down his name, phone number, and a brief message, *'Thanks. How about tea sometime?'*

He handed the clipboard back.

"Thanks," he said.

"I'll make sure Dr. Sunny gets this message," the woman said.

Callum was disappointed but tried not to show it. He smiled at the older woman and got back in the jeep.

He left wondering why he was so disappointed. He wanted to get to know the doctor better.

He waited all day by the telephone, hoping Sunny would call. He ate his solitary supper in the large dining room. Finally, he admitted to himself that she wasn't going to call. The fine Scottish single malt tasted of peat, Highland winds, and rain. It tasted of home. What the heck was he doing here, all by himself, in an empty old house? He belonged in the Highlands with his family and childhood friends. Then he remembered how bored he had been. How everything had become predictable. He could have married young Ella Brown, settled down with a local law practice. He had been on the brink of settling down when he received a notice that his Uncle Mac had left him some money. The only caveat was that he had to travel to India, Mahagiri to be specific, to talk to the Indian attorneys in charge of the old man's estate. Three months ago, he had arrived in Chennai and met with Uncle Mac's attorneys, who had arranged a wire transfer of a generous amount of rupees. In his letter, Mac had urged him to travel around south India and visit Mahagiri. *This was my home for decades*, Mac had written, *go there and breathe the air.* It was not Highland air but it was still a pretty special place, according to Mac. His uncle wanted him to use the money for a new career or job in Mahagiri. *Do it for a bit, and if you don't like it, leave and go back to Scotland,* the old man had written.

His Uncle Mac was right. Mahagiri was a special place. He loved the tea estates, orange and tangerine orchards, the shy native people, and the cool, refreshing air. The crisp breeze made him feel alive. And then he met the lithe doctor. She had made the place even more interesting. Tea would have been the first step. Well, he will just have to visit her again. Maybe tomorrow, he reasoned.

He was about to change and get ready for bed when he heard the phone ring. Who could be ringing so late at night? He rarely had phone calls in the middle of the night. All his business transactions took place during the day. Unless…

He raced down the hallway to the living room, where the phone was still ringing. How many times was that? Five? Or six? He skidded on the wooden floor in his haste as he scooped up the receiver.

"Hallo? Hallo?"

No one replied. Whoever was calling him had hung up. He wondered if it could have been her as he pulled the thick comforter over his shoulder.

CHAPTER TWENTY-SIX

SUNNY AND KAVERI

It had been a long day, and after dinner and a warm bath, I was ready for bed. I was just about to settle down when there was a soft tap on the bedroom door.

"Come in," I called out.

"Dr. Sunny," Girija said as she walked in with a clipboard. "I'm sorry I forgot to give this to you earlier. It slipped my mind."

I took the clipboard from her. I had specifically asked her if there were any new messages, so I knew she wasn't telling me the truth. I looked at the clipboard and read the message from Callum. He had been here while I was away.

I looked up at Girija. "Thank you, Girija; I'll call him tomorrow. I'm too tired now."

I looked again at the message. I remembered his cheeky grin and blue eyes like the Mahagiri summer skies. I mentally shook my head. When did I become a poet? I was about to turn off the light. It was past ten. Was that too late to call?

I threw a blanket over my shoulder and walked into the clinic. I hesitated with my hand on the receiver. Was this a mistake? What was the big deal? It was just an offer to have some tea.

I picked up the phone and dialed his number. It rang and rang. I hung up. It had been a stupid idea to call so late. He was probably already in bed.

Feeling a little down, I went to my room. My last thoughts were of his blue eyes and attractive smile.

The next day, one of my first patients was Kaveri, the older woman who thought she was pregnant. I had previously done a quick test for the pregnancy hormone Human Chorionic Gonadotropin or HCG. As I expected, the result was negative. A blood test was next, but I wanted to talk with her first.

She was sitting in the waiting room, her head and face partially covered by her sari.

"Good Morning," I greeted the woman. "Kaveri, please come with me."

I asked her to disrobe and put on a paper gown. Her vital signs were strong, and her heart and lungs sounded healthy.

"Can you tell me how far along I am?" she asked eagerly.

I smiled at her before replying, "Kaveri, I'm going to show you the inside of your womb with this machine called an ultrasound, alright?"

The machine revealed a mass in her abdomen. It was rather large, about eight or more centimeters long. I sighed to myself.

"Do you see that mass?" I asked, moving the wand over the greyish thing growing in her belly.

She nodded. "Is that my baby?"

"Kaveri, no. There is no heartbeat."

Tears flowed down her cheeks as she looked at the image.

"If it's not a baby, what is it?"

"Something is growing in your stomach," I replied. "You have to go to the hospital so that they can remove it."

"You are sure it's not a baby?" she asked.

"I'm sure. You need to go to the hospital as soon as you can and get it removed. I will contact the hospital and let them know you are coming," I repeated. "It's important you go to the hospital."

She wiped her eyes on the paper gown and wordlessly got up and went to dress behind the wooden screen I had propped up for privacy.

I finished my notes on her chart, and when she came out, fully dressed, I stood up and asked, "Do you need a ride to the hospital? Ragu can take you?"

"No, no. I'll take the bus tomorrow morning."

A couple of days later, I called the hospital to find out her diagnosis. The nurse on duty checked and double-checked, but no one named Kaveri had come in for a test for a stomach tumor.

It was Ragu who brought me the news.

"Dr. Sunny, Kaveri, and her husband are holding a feast tonight to celebrate her late-life pregnancy."

I didn't understand what he was saying for a moment.

"Ragu, I need to go to Kaveri's village," I said. "Let me go talk to Bhadra first. "

Bhadra was seated in her living room, surrounded by a group of women. She looked much healthier. She took one look at my face and asked everyone to leave us.

"What is the matter, Dr. Sunny? I have not had any omens lately."

"Sometimes bad things happen without an omen," I said. "Do you know Kaveri?"

"Yes, she is celebrating good news tonight with a village feast. I'm invited."

"You have to stop it, Bhadra."

Bhadra raised her eyebrows. "Why?"

"I can't share her information. You must stop her. She is not well," I said heatedly.

"I sent her to the hospital for some tests but I called them today and they said she never showed up."

Bhadra was silent for a long moment before looking up at me and asking, "Do you trust me, Dr. Sunny?"

"My mother trusts you and so do I."

She nodded. "Then let me handle it my way."

"What are you going to do?"

"I'm going to a feast tonight."

"But…"

"You said you trusted me."

I sighed.

"You can come too, Dr. Sunny, if you want."

I sat back on the cushions. I knew Bhadra had her own way of managing the village women. Did I trust her enough to let her take care of Kaveri? I wasn't sure of anything.

"Alright, I'll come as your guest," I agreed.

"You must promise not to interfere, even if you don't agree with what I'm doing," Bhadra said. "Promise, Dr. Sunny."

I hesitated before nodding reluctantly.

"I will take care of her," Bhadra said. "I assure you in the end I will not let Kaveri or you down."

I took leave of her, promising to come back later in time for the feast.

Instead of my usual uniform of jeans and shirt, I dressed for the night in a fancy kurta top and matching jewelry. I braided my hair, and Girija insisted that I wear a red rose bud in my hair. I looked at myself in the mirror as she fussed over my hair. My mother and Meena would be proud of my efforts tonight. I was quite aware it was not a happy occasion.

Ragu and Girija accompanied me, and we parked the jeep in front of Bhadra's house. She was waiting for us. She was dressed in a bright red sari. Her hair was loose and flowed down her back.

"Ragu, Dr. Sunny," she said. "We have to drive to Kaveri's house. I'm tired after tying on this sari."

It was a short drive to the other side of the village. Kaveri's house was decorated with strings of lights. Loud film music was being played, and the front yard was filled with people. Everyone stopped to stare as we got out of the jeep. Bhadra was a striking figure. She looked like a goddess come to life.

Kaveri ran out of the house and bowed to touch Bhadra's feet. "Oh, Mother, you have graced my home with your presence."

She introduced a short, bald man as her husband, Singa.

Singa also touched Bhadra's feet. When Kaveri noticed me, she frowned for a second and greeted me with a fake smile.

"Dr. Sunny, I'm so glad to see you. As you can see, I am doing well."

I nodded, but before I could say anything, Bhadra said, "Kaveri, I would like to start the evening with a pooja to bless you and invoke the goddess."

I watched as the women bustled around, following Bhadra's instructions. A deity made of mud and twigs and decorated with white paint was placed on a crude altar. Flowers, fruits, lemons, salt, incense sticks, and several oil lamps made from empty coconut shells were placed before this goddess deity. Bhadra drew a circle around the altar using white rice powder. Everyone stayed clear of this line. However, Bhadra stepped over the line and stood before the deity. In the silence, I could hear the bark of a distant dog. It was twilight, the sacred time of day when it was neither day nor night.

"Welcome. Tonight, we celebrate the Goddess and her bounty. Everyone here knows my devotion to the Goddess. She is light and dark, life and death. Let her power flow into your heart, your body, and your limbs. Welcome her divine force."

As Bhadra spoke, she slowly shuffled from one foot to another. Someone brought a drum and started to pound a deep throbbing rhythm on it. The onlookers picked up the rhythm and started clapping along with the drum beats. Bhadra hummed low in her throat, her feet moving faster and her arms going around in circles. Her hair whipped around her head as she moved, looking like a long black snake.

The onlookers were mesmerized.

"She has been taken over by the goddess," I heard someone say behind me.

I hoped she was well enough for this vigorous dance. Finally, she stopped dancing, her limbs trembling. She looked up, and I saw the lights reflected in her wide-open eyes. She looked eerie and otherworldly. She silently pointed to Kaveri, who trembled and looked frightened.

"Daughter, do not be frightened," Bhadra said in a deep, unfamiliar voice. "Come nearer."

Kaveri was helped into the circle by a couple of women, who immediately left her once she had crossed the white line.

"What do you wish for, daughter?" Bhadra asked.

Kaveri spoke in such a soft whisper that we couldn't hear her, but Bhadra answered.

"Of course, a healthy baby. Come closer."

When Kaveri was right before her, Bhadra laid her two palms on her belly. The crowd watched them in silence. I wondered what Bhadra was doing.

She spoke softly but clearly, "Daughter, this is not a healthy baby. This is not the work of the Goddess."

Kaveri's shoulders shook as she started to weep.

"Cry your tears and offer your sorrow up to the Goddess. She will erase your grief. Let go of the thing in your womb. The Goddess says a child will come to you and Singa, but not from your womb."

I had no idea what Bhadra meant by that last sentence. Kaveri stopped crying and stared at Bhadra with wild hope in her eyes.

"A child will come?" she asked, her voice quaking with emotion.

"Yes, my daughter. You will have your baby by the next full moon."

After she uttered these words, Bhadra collapsed onto the ground. I rushed to check on her. Her pulse was steady, and she seemed to be sleeping. One of the women pushed me aside and said, "This happens after the Goddess enters her. She will sleep for a long time now. Here, help me get her inside."

Several women lifted the sleeping Bhadra and took her inside the house. I saw Kaveri seated on the ground, her head between her hands. I gently rubbed her back. She looked at me, tears glistening on her cheeks.

"Dr. Sunny, you have to help me get this thing out of my womb."

"Of course," I said. "Tomorrow, we'll go to the hospital together."

I didn't know what I witnessed today, but Bhadra and her goddess power were amazing.

CHAPTER TWENTY-SEVEN
SUNNY'S NEW PET

Kaveri's mass turned out to be benign, and soon after her operation, Bhadra came to visit.

"Bhadra, what happened to your prophecy about Kaveri getting a baby?" I asked the older woman.

Girija brought us cups of hot tea and waited to hear Bhadra's answer.

"Well," Bhadra said, taking a sip of tea, "A washerwoman in the village died at childbirth, and her husband couldn't take care of the newborn baby. I introduced him to Kaveri, and now the couple have adopted the infant."

"That was very clever of you," I said, smiling at Bhadra. "How about you? Are you doing all right?"

She nodded. "I am well due to the grace of the goddess who works in mysterious ways."

She added, "I had a vision."

I rolled my eyes. "Another one?"

"Do you still doubt me, Dr. Sunny?" she asked with a smile.

I shook my head.

"Alright. In my vision, I give you a gift."

I started to protest.

She leaned over and took my hands in her large, warm ones.

"My gift to you is Karuta."

"The dog?" I asked, "I don't understand."

"The ways of the gods are inexplicable," Bhadra replied. "In my vision, Lord Yama, the God of Death, told me I had to use my life to help others. An animal needs constant care and companionship, so he wants you to look after this black dog. I will visit her, of course, but she is now yours."

I couldn't talk her out of it, and a few days later, Karuta came to live with me. I shortened her name to Karu, and with her easygoing disposition, she became part of our little family. She quickly learned not to bark at clinic patients. She was very protective of me and barked at anyone knocking on my bedroom door, especially at night.

Once she started to obey my simple commands, she accompanied me on visits to the village. She would patiently wait near the jeep, and once I was done, both of us, along with Ragu, would go for a walk. We loved to stretch our legs before getting back into the jeep.

Karu and I took a hike one bright Sunday morning, the same route where I first saw Callum. As we passed the tea bush where I had found him, I couldn't help looking around.

"Hallo," a voice called.

Karu issued a low warning bark.

"Call off your attack dog; it's me, Callum," he said as he climbed down the embankment.

"Karu, sit," I said. The animal sat on her haunches, looking at the figure approaching us. I also watched him.

He was as handsome as I recalled. He stopped a few paces from us and looked down at the black dog.

"Who is this?"

"This is Karu," I said. The dog wagged her tail when she heard her name. "She was a gift from the God of Death."

Callum looked slightly taken aback and asked, "Seriously? Should I be worried?"

I had to laugh. "No. She is well-behaved and hasn't caused any deaths so far."

He knelt down and let the animal sniff his outstretched hand.

"It's alright, Karu," I said. "He's a friend."

"Hi, Karu. What a beautiful lass you are."

His soft voice and his charming Scottish accent had an effect on me and the dog. As the dog licked his fingers, he stared at me. "Are we friends, though?"

"Yes," I said.

"Then why didn't you call me? Didn't you receive my message?"

I ran my hand over my head and said, "Of course I did. It rang and rang. Then things got crazy at the clinic, and then, well, you know…." I shrugged my shoulders.

Callum nodded with a look of understanding lighting up his face. "Did you, by chance, call late at night?"

I blushed. "Ah, yes, I didn't get the message until then."

"I couldn't move quickly enough to pick up the phone. I had a couple of drinks too many."

"I thought rugby players could run even when drunk," I said teasingly.

He laughed. "Very funny, Doc. Anyway, since you and what was this lass's name again?

"Karu."

"Yes, Karu. You are so close to my home, could you come for that cup of tea?

Karu was looking at Callum with her tongue hanging out. She was clearly besotted, and I could understand her feelings.

"Okay," I said, "Lead the way."

As we walked up the hill, he asked, "So, how have you been?"

"Fine, busy. You know the usual things that happen in a doctor's life."

"Heartbreak and happiness."

I looked at him in surprise and said, "Exactly. In equal parts, How's your hand?"

"Healed, almost," he replied, holding up the hand. There was just a small bandage on it.

"Since I'm here, maybe I can look at it."

"Always a doctor, eh?"

I grinned at him and said, "Can't help myself."

"So, how did the Lord of Death give you a dog?"

I told him about Bhadra.

"She said this dog needed care, and I couldn't refuse a gift from the god," I said.

"She's certainly adorable."

"You like dogs," I said, stating the obvious.

"We always had a couple of hounds lying around. I miss them."

"Well, you can borrow Karu anytime," I said.

"Deal," he said, putting out his hand to shake mine.

I did the same. His hand was warm and firm in mine.

"Wow," I said, looking down at the valley. "You have an incredible view."

"Thank you. This view is the reason I bought the estate because Dorai Raj was a lousy businessman," he said. "Come on,"

The dog pushed me aside and walked up the porch steps.

I laughed and said, "Someone feels at home. Is she okay inside the house?"

"You are thinking like an Indian," he said. "Of course, She can even sleep in the bedroom."

I laughed and said, "She sleeps by my bedside."

"Lucky dog," he muttered.

"What?"

"Nothing. Let's go into the living room. One of these days, I will make it into a library."

He led the way while Karu excitedly walked around, sniffing every corner.

"Karu, come," I said.

"She's okay," he said. "Let her look around."

"Please, sit down," he said. "I'll get us some tea."

I sat down and looked around. The living room seemed to have been decorated by an old British military guy. Military paraphilia hung on the walls, along with swords, old guns, and other weapons. The furniture was mostly wood and leather. The chair by the fireplace wasn't uncomfortable. I could see why Callum thought this room should be a library. One wall was covered with bookshelves. This room reminded me of Mac's living room, just not as cozy or welcoming.

The dog, tired of sniffing furniture legs, sat beside me with a sigh.

"Good girl," I said, patting her soft head.

Callum came in, followed by a woman.

"This is Shanta, my cook and housekeeper," he said.

"And someone who keeps him on task," she said with a smile.

She turned and addressed me, "Dr. Sunny, I've heard all about you. Let me start a fire to make this room cozier."

She looked down at the dog. "And you must be the dog from the God of Death."

Karu looked up and slowly wagged its tail.

She expertly built a fire, and soon, the fireplace had a warm blaze.

"There," she said, dusting her hands. "Come on, girl, Let's find you a treat."

I was surprised when Karu obediently got up and followed the woman.

"Tea, coming in a few minutes, Scot Sir."

"Scot Sir?"

"That's what she calls me. She tried Master, but that sounded something out of *Gone with the Wind*. Scot Sir is what I'm left with."

I giggled. The warm fire felt good.

"So," Callum sat down opposite me "Tell me, Dr. Sunny, have you had a chance to visit your family?"

"Not recently," I said. "They were all here a few months ago. Luckily, I have a phone and computer hooked up now, so I can stay in touch. How about you? Do you miss your family?"

He shook his head and replied, "I do, and I don't. I'm the only son. I have an older sister married to a doctor who lives in London with her two children. I'm a great disappointment to my father. He would like me to marry and settle down in Scotland."

"Why didn't you?"

Before he could reply, the door opened, and Karu came in proudly carrying an old rope in her mouth. She lay down at my feet and began to gnaw on the rope.

"Tea is served, Scott Sir. Would you like me to pour?" Shanta asked.

"I think I can manage," Callum said.

Shanta nodded and left the room. He poured the tea, added a splash of milk, and handed me the cup and saucer.

"How did you know I don't take sugar," I asked.

"Are you kidding? Even Shanta heard about your no-sugar fetish. Apparently, it's the talk of the village."

"Oh," I said, "I was just to remind people it is easy to cut back on sugar. I guess I do sound like a bit of a crusader."

"A bit," he said, grinning at me. "Talking about hating sugar, will you try one of these cardamom biscuits?"

"I don't hate sugar," I said, taking a biscuit. "I say use in moderation."

"Will do, oh great Buddha," he said, teasing me.

The biscuit was fragrant with cardamom and melted in my mouth.

"These are so good," I said, finishing the last bit. "May I have another?"

He passed the plate and said, "Well, Shanta will be happy to hear you approved of her biscuits."

Callum sat back in the chair and looked at me. I stared back, flushing a little at his close scrutiny.

"What? Do I have something stuck in my teeth?" I asked.

He laughed and said, "No, I can't believe you are here. I've been imagining this moment for a while."

"Really? In your imagination, what did we do besides drink tea and stare at one another?"

He grinned and said, "That would be telling. We can walk around the property if you're done with your tea."

I tipped the cup and swallowed the last bit of tea.

"I would love that," I said as I glanced at the sleeping dog, "I bet Karu would, too."

Karu jumped up when she heard her name. It was cool and breezy outside, and we walked up a hill behind the house. There were stupendous views from all sides of the property. From here, I could see the road leading down the hill.

"Does that road go to Mahagiri?" I asked.

"Yes," he said, pointing. "See that huge building on the left side. That is the clubhouse, and beyond that is the golf course. Anyone who's who in Mahagiri comes to golf and dine there."

"What's on the other side of the road?"

He didn't answer for a long moment. I saw him gazing at the horizon, an uneasy look on his face.

"Is it a secret?" I teased.

He laughed and said, ""No, the land is slated for development by the government."

"What kind of development?"

"There will be a government guest house, a park and trail, and a hospital."

I turned to look at him. He looked down at me with a guilty look on his face.

"A hospital. Will it be for the villagers?"

"Yes, and before you ask, I had no idea all it was in the works when I bought this property."

I was puzzled by his attitude. He sounded so defensive.

"I'm not blaming you. Having a hospital would be such a help to the villagers."

He looked relieved. Again, I couldn't understand his behavior.

"I'm glad, Dr. Sunny," he said. "I wasn't sure how you'd take the news about a new hospital."

I shrugged and said, "I think it would be great for the villagers, and you can call me Sunny."

Later, he drove us home in his jeep. As we passed the fancy clubhouse, he turned to me.

"I wonder if you'd like to go to dinner sometime," he asked, gesturing toward the clubhouse. "The chef is quite famous."

"Like a date?" I asked.

"Yes," he said with a grin.

I thought for a moment. There couldn't be any harm in going out for a meal. I had to eat, didn't I?

I nodded and said, "Sure."

"Would this Friday suit you?" he suggested.

"I think so. I rarely plan anything. My calendar is usually empty until a patient shows up."

"I'll pick you up around seven, then?"

I nodded. "Sounds good."

There were no houses or structures on the right side of the road. The landscape was primarily scraggly bushes and tall, thin trees. We then passed a small house.

"Who lives there?" I asked, looking back at the house.

"Interesting story," Callum said. "A chap who thinks he is the protector of the place. According to Shanta, he's called Katu Thatha because he is fiercely protective of the land."

"How did he come to build a house there? Isn't it on government property?" I asked.

"It is, But according to Shanta, the then-collector of the region asked him to stay on the property to keep an eye on vandals and squatters. Of course, now the government wants him to move."

"Is he going to?"

"Yes, he knows he doesn't have any rights."

"What's going to happen to him?"

He shrugged his shoulder and said, "I'm not sure."

Something about the old man living alone and being forced out of the only home he had ever known made me sad and melancholy.

After Callum dropped us at the clinic, I wandered into the living room and sat at the computer. I looked up the proposed development on Club Road. It looked impressive. A local hospital would be great. I wonder if Mother Superior knew about it. I would ask her the next time I see her.

That night, I dreamed of a massive tree with the face of an old man walking down the road.

CHAPTER TWENTY-EIGHT

KATU THATHA

I had not expected to see Callum until Friday evening, so I was surprised when he entered the clinic late Tuesday afternoon with someone in his arms.

"Dr. Sunny," he called out.

I led him into the exam room, where he gently laid down the old man he was carrying. The man had a long, wispy beard and thick grey hair.

"This is Katu Thatha," Callum said, wiping his brow. "I found him on the side of the road. There are no apparent injuries, At least none I could see."

I examined the older man. He had a steady but faint pulse, and no overt injuries or wounds were on him. I tapped him gently on the cheeks.

"Thatha, wake up," I said.

He sighed, and finally, his eyelids fluttered open.

"Eh, What? Where am I?" he said softly, slurring his words.

"Katu Thatha," I said, leaning down. "You are at the clinic. I'm Dr. Sunny."

A drip of salvia rolled down his chin. His right side was definitely droopy. A stroke?

"It looks like you may have had a stroke," I said. "I'm going to give you some medicine, but I need your permission."

He nodded and closed his eyes. I started an IV.

"Will he be alright?" Callum asked.

His Scottish accent was very pronounced. He sounded distraught.

"We have to wait and see If we caught the stroke in time. He should recover, But he will need care and monitoring for the next few days."

"I can drive him to the mission where he can receive the care he needs," Callum offered.

"Alright, let's wait an hour or so. I want to make sure he is stable before you take him. Can you call Mother Superior and tell her you are bringing in a stroke patient?"

He nodded and walked out of the exam room.

"Wait," I called out, hurrying after him. "Girija will be happy to get you a cup of tea. You can wait in my living room."

He smiled and nodded again. I watched him walk away.

An hour later, he drove off with the old man, and I turned my attention to my other patients.

CHAPTER TWENTY-NINE
CALLUM (DATE NIGHT)

C allum changed his shirt twice and returned to the original blue one.

"You are a nervous man," Shanta said with a chuckle as she ironed the shirt for the second time.

"I want to make a good impression," he said, buttoning his cuffs.

He shrugged into a dark blue sports coat and ran his fingers through his hair. He probably needed a haircut soon.

"You look beautiful," Shanta said teasingly.

He glared at her.

"I just want…"

"Yes, you'll make a good impression; don't worry. Doctor Sunny was making googly eyes at you; didn't you notice?"

Callum stared at his housekeeper.

"No, I didn't," he said. "Anyway, shouldn't you be dusting or something?"

He ignored her laughter. He arrived at the clinic to find Ragu waiting on the front steps. What was going on? Had she changed her mind?

"Scot Sir," Ragu said in a polite voice.

Here it comes. Sunny was bailing.

"Just wanted to make sure you understand that Dr. Sunny is my responsibility."

"What?"

This was not what he expected Ragu to say.

"Scot Sir, we, Girija and I, just want to say that Dr. Sunny is exceptional and…."

"Ragu," Sunny's voice interrupted whatever the older man was about to say. "Do you need something?"

"Nothing, Dr. Sunny," Ragu said with a guilty look. "I was just wishing Scot Sir a good evening."

"I'll be back soon," Sunny said with a sharp look in Ragu's direction. "I told Girija not to wait up for me. Just make sure Karu is let out before you turn in."

"Of course, Dr. Sunny," Ragu said.

The dog came down the steps, wagging her tail.

"Hey there, lass," Callum squatted down to pet the dog. "You must stay here and keep the Ragu and his missus safe, okay?"

Sunny waited until Callum stood up and said, "Karu, inside Now."

The dog gave a little whimper but obeyed. She stood on the porch steps, looking like she had been abandoned.

"You must be heartless to leave that wee lass," Callum said.

"She'll be fine. She is a little spoiled and used to coming with me everywhere."

Sunny waved to the couple and climbed into the jeep.

He glanced at his passenger. "You clean up nicely."

She blushed. "Thank you. You clean up well too, Callum. This is just an old sari."

The old sari was a beautiful turquoise with silver threads woven into it. The matching blouse was tied together in the back with silver tassels. She had a bright blue bindi dot on her forehead and matching silver earrings, necklace, and bangles. She smelled like fresh jasmine.

At the clubhouse, he parked the jeep and came around to help her out. She had already opened the car door and was just stepping out.

They walked into the fancy lobby of the club. A miniature waterfall on one wall and a large mirror on the other made the room seem even more spacious.

"Wow," she said. "This is grand."

"Dinner for two?" a uniformed man asked them, "Do you have reservations?"

"Never mind, I'll take care of them," said an elderly gentleman sporting a massive white mustache and fancy turban. "Mr. Callum, Welcome, sir."

"Mukherjee, how are you?" Callum shook the man's hand. "Thanks for stepping in, but I did have a reservation."

"I know, Mr. Callum. I saw your name in the book. Come, come, I have a special table for you and your young lady."

He bowed. "Dr. Sunny, you are always welcome."

"Oh, thank you." Sunny smiled, "And please, it's Sunny."

"You have earned the title Doctor," the man said. "My name is Mukherjee. I'm the head waiter. Please follow me."

He led them to an alcove right by the fireplace.

"Two glasses of champagne?"

"No, thank you," Sunny said. "Mineral water for me."

"Same here," Callum said.

"Still or bubbly?"

"Still is fine," Sunny said.

"Very well, the waiter will be here shortly. Enjoy your meal, sir, Dr. Sunny."

Sunny looked around and then at Callum, who was staring at her.

"What?'

He shook his head. "I can't believe you are here. I was afraid you'd cancel at the last minute, And you look beautiful."

She blushed. "Thank you, Ah, here's the waiter."

CHAPTER THIRTY
SUNNY (DATE NIGHT)

I f anyone had asked me later what we had for dinner, I wouldn't have been able to tell them. Dinner was a blur because I was enchanted and enamored. I found Callum to be funny and entertaining. I couldn't help thinking how much I wanted my family to meet him. I was sure they would like him too. He was handsome and charming. Yes, I'm sounding like a smitten schoolgirl.

"Sunny is an unusual name. Is it a nickname?" he asked, taking a bite of salad.

I nodded. "Yes, it is. My mother calls me Thangam. When I was in kindergarten, I liked to wear this yellow raincoat and boots, and one day...."

He interrupted, astonished, "You fell off the jungle gym."

I gaped at him. "How did you know?"

We both stared at each other and then burst out laughing in unison.

"It was you," we both said at the same time.

"Yes," he said. "You were lying on there, looking like a sunny-side up egg."

"Egg?" I asked sharply, "I thought I was as sunny as the yellow sun."

He laughed. "No, no. More like an egg splattered on the playground."

I wrinkled my nose. "Well, that's not how I remember it."

He grinned at me. "Still, the name suits you."

"You were in India and Mahagiri?" I asked him in astonishment.

"Yes," he said, "But I barely remember much about that visit. We were visiting a tea plantation in Mahagiri. I would have attended the local school, but my father had to return to Scotland."

"You were in school only for one day?" I asked, "And I met you, and you gave me a nickname?"

"I guess I used my time well," he said with his familiar grin.

I couldn't help grinning back.

We finished dinner, hardly noticing the time.

"I think we better get you back before Ragu sends out a search party," Callum said, looking at his watch.

As he drove, he glanced at me. "I hope we can do this again. Maybe even go to Lower Mahagiri."

I was glad he couldn't see me blushing in the semi-darkness of the moving vehicle.

"That sounds great," I replied, "Though I'm not sure there are such fancy places down there."

"Oh, I'll find something."

The drive ended way too soon for me. We sat for a moment in the jeep, and I felt we were the only people in the world.

"Sunny," he said, turning toward me, "I have something to tell you."

"Yes?"

I turned, and our faces were close. I looked into Callum's eyes, which were a deep navy blue in the dark. The moment was ripe with possibility.

"Dr. Sunny," a knuckle wrapping on the passenger side of the jeep startled me.

I jumped a little, feeling guilty. It was Ragu trying to peer inside.

"Move aside, Ragu," I said through the glass. "I'm getting out."

He moved away from the car door, and I stepped out. I saw Karu wagging her tail and Girija standing on the porch with a very sour look. I sighed.

Callum came around and bent down to pet Karu.

He looked up at me. "See you soon, Dr. Sunny."

"Yes, see you," I said. "Thank you for a lovely dinner."

"You're welcome. It was my pleasure."

I walked up to the porch and turned to watch him drive away. He raised his hand, and I waggled my fingers at him. I wasn't sure he could see my gesture in the dark. The dog followed me, and I went into the bedroom, firmly shutting the door behind me. I knew Ragu and Girija were looking out for me, but tonight, I didn't want to explain anything to them. When I heard a soft knock on the door, I pretended to be asleep and didn't get up.

CHAPTER THIRTY-ONE
SUNNY (SURPRISES AT HOME)

S unday dawned bright and clear. I looked forward to visiting my mother on Sunday with Ragu and Girija. Of course, Karu jumped in as soon as I opened the jeep door. She wasn't going to be left behind this time.

There was a sharpness in the air, winter wasn't far away. The only sounds in the jeep were Karu's soft, excited dog woofs; it was her way of asking if we were there yet.

"Dr. Sunny," Girija broke the silence.

I half turned from the passenger side to look back at her with a questioning look.

"Dr. Sunny," she said again, "We didn't mean to meddle in your affairs last night."

I sighed inwardly.

"I know, Girija," I said. "I'm not angry with you or Ragu. You have my best interests at heart. You must remember I'm nearly twenty-eight years old, a doctor, and your employer."

She had an unhappy look. "I know, Dr. Sunny," she said, "I have come to think of you as my own daughter."

I smiled to soften my words. "Thank you, Girija. That is so sweet of you, One mother is quite enough for me."

Ragu laughed. "And she is quite the mother, Dr. Sunny. Little Mother is not one you want to mess with."

We all laughed, and the tension lessened.

I asked, "Why are you so protective of me? Don't you trust me or Callum?"

There was a long silence, and finally, Girija spoke up.

"I met his housekeeper, Shanta, at the local market, and she said her master has a girl back in Scotland."

I was surprised. No, I was shocked. But I kept my voice casual. "What else did you hear?"

Ragu answered now, "Not a lot of details except he's betrothed to her, and she calls every night, asking for Scot Sir."

I sighed to myself. Things were always complex.

"I'm glad you told me," I said stiffly.

I saw Ragu glance at his wife through the rearview mirror, but the couple said nothing more. We drove in silence until we pulled in front of my mother's house, my childhood home. Unsurprisingly, a greeting party was waiting for us by the open gate. Bindita was jumping up and down in excitement. Meena, Devi, my mother, and Bhojan were also waiting.

Ragu stopped the jeep. I hugged Bindita and greeted everyone. Karu was going crazy in the jeep, wanting to be let out. I had brought a leash because I was unsure whether the puppy would behave. But I needn't have worried. Karu was gentle with the youngster, licking her face and greeting everyone with a wagging tail and a huge grin.

"Come on, Girija, let me get you a cup of tea," Devi said, taking hold of Girija's arm. They disappeared into the kitchen area.

Bhojan and Ragu wandered off to walk in the orchards, and I looked at Bindita, Meena, and my mother.

I hugged my mother and whispered, "I'm so glad to see you."

"Are you alright?" she asked, looking at me with sharp eyes.

"Of course, I am," I answered. "Just a little tired. Let's go to the memorial."

"I'll take the dog and Bindita to the front yard," Meena said. "Raj is supposed to come soon. He has a meeting but promised to be here for lunch."

I watched the three of them walk away.

"They all have a lot of energy," I said wistfully.

"You have been working too hard," my mother said. "Can't you take a short holiday?"

I shook my head and said, "Not right now. There is too much going on."

She slid her arm through my elbow, and we walked to the back of the house. A few roses were still in full bloom. We stood together, staring at the stone structure.

"I still miss him, you know," my mother said, her voice soft. "True love is a true wonder."

I hugged her. I wanted to tell her about Callum and ask her advice. I didn't want to talk about my life. Instead, we shared memories of my father as we returned to the kitchen.

"There you are, *kutty*," Devi said, handing me a cup of tea. I could smell the fragrant cardamom and ginger.

"You know, Devi, the mission has a garden where they grow all kinds of herbs, and I've tasted some interesting teas," I said, blowing on the hot liquid before taking a sip. "I'll see if I can bring you some next time. There are flavors like lavender mint and geranium rose."

"I have never heard of these teas," Devi said. "How are you doing, *kutty*?"

I smiled at her. She had known me all my life, and I would be a *kutty* in her eyes, even if I was sixty!

"I've been busy. A doctor's job is never done. Girija and Ragu take good care of me."

Girija looked up from chopping carrots and potatoes.

"Hmm," she said, "You do need looking after. If I don't insist, she won't eat."

Devi turned to her with her own story about my eating hab-its. I quietly slipped out of the kitchen.

My mother was seated on the front porch watching Bindita. Karu was seated beside her.

"Are you having fun?" I asked the dog, who wagged its tail and then ran back to Bindita.

Meena came and sat down next to us.
"That was Raj on the phone. He says he's bringing a guest for lunch."

My mother got up. "I'll tell Devi."

Meena bumped my shoulder and asked, "How are you, sis? Tell me the truth now."

"I'm fine," I said. "Just working hard."

"Okay," Meena said, "Remember, I'm your *chechi*, and you can tell me anything."

"You hated it when I called you *chechi*." I retorted back.

She laughed, and I joined her.

"Yeah, I do remember," she said. "You were always following me around and getting in the way."

"And you were a big sister with big plans," I said.

"I can't get over how grown up you are," she said. "Soon, we'll be marrying you off."

"No thanks," I said quickly. "No seeing ceremony for me."

"You could have more than one like me," she said with a chuckle.

We were silent, remembering her various ceremonies. I was more dressed up than Meena at her first seeing ceremony.

We heard a car drive up and into the driveway.

"Papa," Bindita yelled as she rushed to greet her father. Karu wasn't far behind, racing along with her.

I stood up to follow them. I didn't want Karu to run out of the open gate. I heard the murmur of male voices. Raj's car was parked right behind the jeep. His back was toward me; he was talking to someone, gesturing with his arms. Raj turned, and then I saw he was talking to Callum. My breath froze in my chest, and I stood absolutely still, unsure what to do. I wanted to talk to him, but certainly not at my mother's house. Things were going to get complicated fast.

CHAPTER THIRTY-TWO
SUNNY WAITS FOR AN EXPLANATION

What was Callum doing here?

Raj had no idea I already knew Callum as he introduced me to him with enthusiasm.

"This is Callum Nigel MacPherson," he said. "He's Mac's nephew from Scotland."

I cleared my throat and said, "Actually, I know Mr. Macpherson, we've met."

I avoided looking at Callum directly but couldn't help glancing at him sideways. He looked distressed, and his face was a bright red. I was glad to see he was embarrassed. I waited for him to offer an explanation.

Raj looked at me and then Callum, confusion on his face.

"How? Do you...."

"Raj," Callum's voice was hoarse. He cleared his throat, "Sunny and I know each other well. We've..."

I interrupted him before he could say anything more. "He's come to the clinic for a hand injury."

"Oh." Raj's face cleared, though he still looked a bit perplexed. "Is your hand better?"

Callum answered, "Yes, it's fine."

Raj nodded. "Let me go say hello to Meena and Amma. Sunny, can you show Callum to the living room."

When he left, I looked at Callum, waiting for an explanation.

"Sunny," he almost groaned aloud, "I'm sorry. I meant to tell you I was Mac's nephew. But there was never a good time."

"Really?" my voice was cold. It reminded me of my mother's angry tone. I stood up straighter, unconsciously mimicking her. "Not even when you held my hand on the way back from our date. Or when you were giving me a taste of the fruit tart. Or...."

"Okay, okay, I get it," he ran his fingers through his hair. "I'm a cad. What can I say?"

I wanted to laugh. A cad? How like him to take this to the next comical level.

"Yes, a cad," I agreed. He looked even gloomier.

He didn't know I knew about his girlfriend back in Scotland. He had much explaining to do, but now was not the time.

I turned on my heel and started toward the house. I didn't look back to see whether he was following me. I heard the crunch of gravel behind me.

The dining room was filled with people and noisy conversation. The air was fragrant with fried spices, warm ghee, and hot food. It had a delicious aroma, but I had no appetite. I wanted to go into my old bedroom, get under the covers, and hide.

My mother and Meena greeted and welcomed Callum.

My mother stared at Callum. "You look a bit like a young Mac," she said. "Raj says we'll be seeing more of you. I'm so glad; it's like having a bit of Mac back again."

He smiled at my mother. "Little Mother, I've heard all about you."

My mother was charmed, I could tell.

She said with a laugh, "All the stories are exaggerated. Come sit down."

I bit my lip and said nothing.

Meena was also effusive in her greeting, "Callum. What a lovely name."

"What does Callum mean?" Raj asked, helping himself to the potatoes and greens dish.

"It's a Celtic/Gaelic name, rather old-fashioned, and means dove, a symbol of purity and peace for early Christians. Some say it also means a follower of St. Columba."

"That is great," Meena replied. "Our names all have meanings too."

This led to a long discussion about all our names and meanings.

"You have to hear how Sunny named herself," Meena said with a laugh.

"It's not that great a story," I mumbled.

"Nonsense," Raj said. "It's hilarious."

"When she was young, she loved to wear a yellow raincoat and matching boots," Meena said. "Anyway, the story goes that she was goofing around on the monkey bars and fell down one day. A young foreign boy helped her up and nicknamed her Sunny. She insisted we call her Sunny from that day."

Callum looked around us and said, "I was the boy who helped her up."

"Wait, What? You were the boy in the playground?" Meena asked.

There was a gasp from my mother.

Meena looked around the table in astonishment.

"Sunny, what are the odds of this?" Meena asked me. She turned to Callum and continued, "I can't believe this. We have been teasing her about this imaginary boy who named her, and here you are in the flesh."

I could feel a blush creeping up my neck, and I said nothing.

"Wait, Sunny, did you know it was Callum?" my mother asked. She didn't miss a thing, my mother.

I swallowed and replied, "Yes, I found out a few days ago. I was pretty surprised, too."

My mother stared at me, and I shifted in my seat. I was glad when Callum spoke up.

"What does Thangam mean?" Callum asked.

"Oh, that is her other nickname, golden or precious," my mother replied. "I always loved that name and thought it suited her."

"No, it doesn't," Meena said. "It should have been One Who Has Her Nose Stuck in a Book."

Everyone laughed, and I awkwardly joined in, my lips feeling a little stiff. Only I heard Callum mutter under his breath, "precious as gold."

I blushed and concentrated on eating carrots tossed in caraway seeds and jaggery.

I just started to relax and enjoy the food when Girija entered the dining room carrying a plate of freshly made rotis.

CHAPTER THIRTY-THREE
CALLUM (SECRET IS OUT)

H e felt like a fraud for sitting down and eating the meal when he only wanted to apologize to Sunny and beg her forgiveness. He wanted to drag her out of the room and explain until she looked him in the eye with the same twinkle she had when they were at the clubhouse. Instead, he concentrated on answering questions about Scotland and his family.

Then Girija walked in with a plate of hot bread, and the world came to a standstill. They stared at each other with shocked expressions.

"What are you staring at, Callum?" Little Mother asked. She turned and saw Girija standing in the doorway. "Come on in, Girija, the rotis will get cold. As you can see, we have a guest for lunch today."

Girija walked up to the table, disapproval written on her face.

"What's the matter with you?" Meena asked. "You look like you've eaten a sour orange."

Girija placed the plate of rotis on the table but misjudged the distance, and the plate clattered to the floor. Everyone looked at her in surprise. She bent down and picked up the plate. Her face was a mask of distress and horror.

"I'm so sorry," she said. "I'll bring fresh ones."

"What is the matter with her?" Meena asked again when Girija had left the dining room. "She's gone completely bonkers."

There was a moment of silence, and as of one, everyone turned to look at Callum.

"So, Callum, you are the new addition to our table, and Girija seemed upset to see you. Can you explain?" Little Mother asked him.

He looked a little desperate. Sunny spoke up.

"Amma," she said. "This is my fault."

Everyone turned to look at her, and he saw a blush creeping up her neck and face.

"A few days ago, I went to dinner with Callum...."

"Dinner?" Meena interrupted. "What do you mean?"

She was about to continue, but Callum interrupted.

"Little Mother, Raj, Meena, I met Sunny when I had an infection in my hand. She cleaned the wound and took me to the mission to heal, and as a thank-you for her care, I wanted to do something and so took her out to dinner."

When he finished, there was a deep silence, and it seemed to be there was a collective sigh of relief. What were they expecting? Something torrid?

Her mother looked at him and Sunny, who still looked mortified.

Finally, she spoke up,

"Thangam, this sounds perfectly innocent. Secrets have a way of coming out."

She waited for Sunny to speak up.

"Yes, Amma. Although it wasn't really a secret."

"Well," Meena started to say, but Raj poked her. "What? Okay, okay."

Meena started to stand up. "I'll go talk to Girija."

My mother also stood up. "Meena, please serve the pudding and ice cream. Sunny, can you come with me?"

Callum watched helplessly as they walked out of the dining room. *Secrets have a way of coming out.*

CHAPTER THIRTY-FOUR
SUNNY (IN THE ORCHARD)

I followed my mother down the familiar corridor to the kitchen. She stopped midway and turned to me.

"What is going on, Thangam? This is not like you to keep secrets and tell...."

I interrupted her. "Amma, it's nothing like that. It was totally innocent. Girija overacted when she saw Callum. She didn't think I should go out to dinner."

My mother stared at me. I almost spoke up to fill the silence, but my mother said, "Thangam, you are a grown woman and a qualified doctor, I don't want to tell you what to do. But just be careful."

I nodded, relieved. "I will, Amma. I promise."

My mother said nothing more and we walked into the kitchen where Girija and Devi were huddled in front of the hearth, having a hushed conversation.

"Girija," my mother took command, as always. "Thangam has told us she knows Mr. Callum and went to dinner with him."

Girija nodded, still looking upset. "We were just trying to look out for her."

Before she could go on, I said, "Girija, I've told Amma everything, and you don't have to worry anymore."

She smiled, and her expression cleared. She came up to me and gave me a brief hug. "Thank the Goddess, you have come clean."

I was annoyed at her words. There was nothing to come clean about and I said sharply, "Perhaps you should make sure Bhojan and Ragu have some lunch. We'll have to leave in a couple of hours."

"So soon?" Devi came up to me, "We hardly see you anymore."

"I know, Devi. It's been crazy at the clinic. Hopefully, I'll be able to take some time off soon and relax."

I fed Karu, who had followed us into the kitchen and joined everyone in the dining room.

I avoided my mother's eyes. She was too sharp. I also avoided looking at Callum. This attraction between us had to stop. It would only bring trouble and heartbreak.

The ice cream had been served, and Bindita was full of sugar energy. I offered to take her for a walk.

"Karu needs exercise, too. We can go to the orchard," I said.

"Perhaps you can show me around?" Callum said.

He looked at me with an innocent expression.

"Sure," I tried to sound off-hand and casual, avoiding Meena's amused stare.

Soon, the two of us, Bindita and the dog, crossed the street to enter the fruit orchard.

The orchard is a special place filled with green tranquility and incredible fruit. Karu was having a blast running between the trees, which seemed taller and thicker than the last time I had visited them. The pear trees were laden with fruit. These round, crunchy pears were called "pot pears," perhaps because of their shape. They weren't as popular as the creamy soft pears, but our family loved the crunch, and every fall, my mother made jars of pale-yellow jam. I reached up and picked one and wiped it on the end of my tunic before biting into the juicy fruit.

"Can I have a pear?" Bindita asked.

"Of course," Callum reached up and plucked one. He wiped the dust off the fruit with his shirt before giving it to her.

She ran ahead, stopping now and then to take a bite of the pear. I kept an eye on her.

I looked up to see Callum watching me.

"I'm sorry," he said. "I should have told you I was Mac's nephew."

"Why didn't you?" I asked, my mouth full of sweet pear bits.

He shook his head. "I really don't know what I was thinking. I wanted to tell you, but every time I started to say something, it was like a huge lump in my throat was preventing me from speaking."

"You should speak to a doctor about that lump."

He smiled at me. "You're not angry?"

I threw the pear core away. "Not about this. I heard a rumor that you are engaged to a Scottish girl. Girija and Ragu were quite concerned about me spending time with you."

He ran his fingers through his hair. "No wonder they were so suspicious of me. You must think me a real cad now."

"My mother always told me not to listen to gossip because it is almost always untrue."

He sighed with relief and said, "Your mother is right. I'm not engaged to anyone. I may know who started this rumor. Shanta must have overheard me talking to my mother. She's been calling and wanting to know when I'm returning home. She wants me to get married and settle down.

"All I want to do is live in Mahagiri, and this business idea seemed like a way to make it happen. After meeting you, I have another reason to want to stay in here."

"What? So, it's my fault?"

"Of course not," he ran his fingers through his hair again.

I decided to stop teasing him. I took his hand in mine.

"It's okay, Callum. I believe you. Come on, let's find Karu and Bindita."

It was a pleasant afternoon; the sun was warm on my back, and I was happy to be with Callum. We found Bindita sitting down under a large plum tree. Karu was seated next to her, panting in the shade.

"This is the famous tree where Mac rescued Meena," I said.

He looked up at the large tree. "Really? It looks big."

"Well, it happened a few years ago. One afternoon, Mac found Meena crying in this tree because she was scared to get down. He talked her down and soon became part of the family."

He squeezed my hand. "I'm glad he did. Are you okay with me going into business with Meena and Raj?"

I squeezed his hand back. "Yes, of course."

"And you believe me about not being engaged?"

"Yes," I assured him. "I believe you. Besides, Girija and Ragu will always be there to protect my honor."

"I know they will."

"Come on, you two," I said as we descended the slope.

We had reached the bottom of the orchard, where tea bushes replaced the trees. We all stopped to stare down into the valley below us.

"That is a deep valley," Bindita said.

I sighed at the pretty picture in front of us.

"It's a beautiful and special place," Callum said softly.

Bindi interrupted our moment. "Look, Karu is running away."

"Come back, Karu," I yelled, giving chase to the dog. She went down the hill toward a man struggling with a bundle in his arms.

He looked exhausted and relieved when he saw us.

"Miss, Sir, you have to help my daughter," he said. He laid the bundle he was carrying down on the ground before us. I immediately sat on my haunches and pulled aside the sheet to see a small girl about ten years old. Her face was puffed and swollen, covered with bites.

"What happened to her?" I asked the man.

"Bees," the man sobbed. "I told her repeatedly not to climb the tree behind our house because of the bees, but she never listens. I found her like this, lying on the ground. I didn't know what to do."

I placed a calming hand on his shoulder. "I'm a doctor. Let me take a look."

"A doctor? Here in the orchard? God is good today."

I didn't say anything because it didn't look good. The girl's pulse was thready and thin. I wish I had my medical bag. She had multiple stings on her face, neck and arms. I rolled her on her side and examined the back of her head. I touched it and felt a large lump. She must have hit her head when she fell out of the tree. A concussion?

"Callum, do you have your wallet with you?"

"Yes," he pulled it out.

"Give me a credit card?"

I used the card to scrape away as many stingers as I could.

"We need to get her to the hospital."

Even before I finished speaking, Callum was running up the slope.

"I'll have the jeep waiting for you," he shouted over his shoulder.

Bindita put her hand on my shoulder, reminding me she was still with me.

"It's alright, Bindita," I said. "We'll take care of her."

I turned to the father, who was weeping silently. "What is your name?"

"Dinesh," he said, wiping his cheeks. "This is Arti."

"Arti," I patted her cheek, "Wake up."

She opened her eyes, looking at me and then her father.

"My face hurts," she whimpered.

"You have been stung by many bees," I said. "I'm going to take you to the hospital where they will help you. You must be a brave girl, Arti."

The father picked up the girl and started up the slope. I held Bindita's hand as we walked past the plum and pear trees. The late afternoon shadows looked menacing, and I shivered.

True to his word, Callum had the jeep waiting for us by the orchard gate. Girija and Ragu were waiting beside the vehicle.

Meena crossed the street, and Bindita ran into her arms.

"Mommy," she said with a whimper.

"She's okay," I told Meena. "She's upset to see the state of this little girl. Bindita, I'll be back soon. You go inside and have some ice cream. Doctor's orders, okay?"

Bindita nodded; her face still pressed into Meena's shoulder.

I looked over to where my family was gathered. I waved and yelled, "We'll come back soon."

My mother yelled across the street, "You go on, *kutty,* and take care of the girl."

Callum said, "Ragu can drive you to the hospital. I'll follow you."

"There's no need, Callum," I said. "I'll talk to you later tonight."

Feeling everyone's eyes, I smiled and jumped in the jeep. Ragu got us to the hospital in record time, and soon, the girl was on histamines and pain medications. Once she was settled, I turned to leave.

"Doctor, thank you," Dinesh had followed me out into the hospital corridor. "Little Mother speaks of you often. I should have recognized you."

I smiled and said, "I'm glad Arti will be fine, and I was there to help."

He nodded and pressed my hands in thanks.

Ragu and Girija were waiting for me. Darkness was falling fast as we drove home to the clinic. The black velvet sky was dotted with twinkling stars. It was a vast universe out there, and I felt like a tiny, insignificant star.

After dinner and a bath, I was ready for bed. I waited until Girija finished tidying up, and when she finally closed the living room door, I got up and walked into the exam room to use the phone. This time, it rang only once before Callum picked it up.

CHAPTER THIRTY-FIVE
CALLUM AND LITTLE MOTHER

He knew Sunny was an extraordinary doctor, but it was something else to watch her work. She had been so calm and collected. It was hard not to freak out at seeing the child's swollen face. Sunny had been in her element, taking charge of the situation.

When he had gone to take leave of her family, he found Little Mother waiting for him.

"I'll walk you out," she said.

"So, Callum, how are you settling in?"

He looked a little surprised by the question.

"Fine, Little Mother," he said. "Everyone has been kind."

"Especially my daughter, Thangam?"

Again, he was taken aback by her straightforwardness. This was a fearless mother defending her young.

"Yes, she also has been kind to me," he picked his words carefully. "I was amazed today, watching her work with the girl."

"She has always been a careful, meticulous person," replied Little Mother. "She is good at what she does. She was a good student, but she is still very naïve about affairs of the heart."

This was not what he was expecting. He said nothing, and she continued.

"I must ask you to be careful in your actions in the coming days and weeks. I don't want Thangam hurt."

He took a deep breath. "Little Mother, you don't have anything to fear from me. I have only your daughter's best interests at heart. I would never do anything to jeopardize her career or reputation."

The tiny woman turned and stared at him, her deep brown eyes searching the very depths of his soul. Finally, what she saw must have satisfied her because she gave a sharp nod.

"Have a safe drive home," she said, touching his arm softly. "I suppose we'll see you again?"

"Yes, thank you for a delicious lunch."

She nodded gravely. He left her standing by the front gate, a vigilant guardian of her family.

He remembered his words as he picked up the ringing phone. He knew right away it was Sunny.

"Hey, there," he answered. "How's your patient?"

"She's going to be fine," she sighed.

"Long day?" he asked.

"Yes, it was. I wish I could have said a proper goodbye to my mother."

"Well, I said it for you," he said dryly.

She laughed. "Did she lecture you?"

"Not really."

"You can't fool her, you know."

"She just wanted to make sure I wouldn't hurt you."

There was a long pause.

Finally, she spoke, "What did you say?"

"I, of course, have no intention of hurting you, so that's what I said."

"I'm glad you all talked about me when I wasn't there," her tone was dry.

"It wasn't like that at all. She walked me to the gate and said a few words. She doesn't mince words, your mother."

"No, she is very straightforward. You get what you see."

"I like that because I like to think I'm like that too."

"Hmmm. On the other hand, I'm dark and mysterious," Sunny giggled.

He loved her laugh. It made her sound so young.

"So, Ms. Dark and Mysterious, are you up for a weekend hike and picnic?"

"Yes," she said. "I would love that."

"Good, I'll call mid-week to finalize?"

"Sounds good."

After they said goodnight, he slowly returned the phone receiver, thinking about her. He sat back in the chair and stared at the cold fireplace. He thought about his conversation with Little Mother. Of course, he didn't want to hurt Sunny. He wanted her in his life. Did he want to marry?

He remembered what his mother had said to him when he was dating Ella.

"Callum," she said in her heavy Scottish accent. "You shouldn't imagine life with Ella. Rather, ask yourself if you can live *without* her. That is the question you should be asking."

She was right, as always. He left Ella without a thought when he received Uncle Mac's letter. Was Sunny just a rebound from

Ella? She couldn't be because Ella didn't mean that much to him. Ella was definitely in his past.

Could he live without Sunny? That was the 64-million-dollar question.

CHAPTER THIRTY-SIX
SUNNY AND SISTER CLARICE

The thought of the upcoming hike and picnic kept me going.

Late in the day, I received a call from the mission. Mother Superior wanted me to come by and see a patient.

"Who is it, Mother?"

She sighed out loud. "It's Sister Clarice, I'm afraid. She has been ill for some time. We have been treating her pancreatic cancer with herbs, but now she needs stronger medicine."

I was sorry to hear this about the nun and promised to come by as soon as I finished at the clinic.

"Come and stay for supper," the nun said before hanging up.

I walked to the kitchen to tell Girija my evening plans.

"Would you like to come with us to the mission?" I asked her.

She was boiling milk for afternoon tea. She turned off the heat and looked at me, "I think I'll stay here. Karu can keep me company, and I'll make a simple dinner for myself."

Once I had seen the last patient, I joined Girija in the kitchen for tea and cake.

It was already getting dark when Ragu and I set off for the mission.

"Do you know how old Sister Clarice is?" I asked Ragu.

He shrugged his shoulders. "I don't think she ever mentioned it. The sister always said age is just a number."

"I'm afraid she is bad off," I said. "I hope she's not suffering."

A novice awaited me to the mission clinic, and I followed her. Sister Clarice had been a large woman. I was surprised at how she had deteriorated since I had seen her last. I sat down next to her and gently felt her pulse. At my touch, she opened her eyes.

"Dr. Sunny," she said in a soft voice. "Things must be bad indeed if they called you in."

I smiled at her. "Hello, sister. I'm glad to see you, but sorry you aren't feeling too well."

"Oh, are you here to give me some medicine?"

"That depends on how you are feeling?"

I looked over her chart. She was in the final stages of pancreatic cancer.

"Dr. Sunny, can I talk to you for a moment?" Mother Superior said from the doorway.

"I'll be right back," I said to Sister Clarice as I followed Mother Superior to the corridor.

"Thank you for coming, Dr. Sunny," she said. Her face and demeanor were grave. "As you read in her charts, she had been diagnosed with cancer well over a year ago. She was doing well until a few weeks ago. The pain seems to have worsened, and valerian and other roots don't help anymore."

I nodded and said, "I'll start her on a morphine drip."

"She's saying she doesn't want anything for the pain," the nun said.

"Why is that?"

"You know, we believe that suffering is part of life and must be faced with stoicism, but I believe God will not want any of His children to suffer needlessly."

I couldn't agree more and said, "Perhaps both of us can talk her into it?"

She sighed and said, "She is very stubborn. Maybe it's best to say nothing about morphine right now."

I frowned. I didn't like to deceive my patient.

I tried to be diplomatic. "Perhaps I can talk to her and see what she says."

"Alright," the nun sounded tired. "I'll be in the parlor."

I went back inside and sat down by the sick nun. She was pale, and I could see lines of pain ingrained on her forehead and cheeks.

"Are you in a lot of pain, Sister Clarice?"

She opened her eyes. "No, dear. Nothing like what Christ suffered for us on the cross."

I took her hand in mine. They were work-hardened with calluses on the palms and bases of the fingers. These fingers had coaxed countless plants and herbs to grow and nourish. I wanted to help ease her pain. She deserved to rest.

"Sister, can I give you an IV? Some fluid would help you."

She looked at me and said, "You want to give me morphine."

I replied, "I guess I can't fool you, Sister."

We smiled at each other. Her smile was weary and tinged with pain.

"If you take just a little bit of morphine, it might help you attend the evening prayer service."

Her eyes brightened. "Really? That would be lovely. Perhaps you can give just a little to help me get to the chapel for prayers."

I placed an IV and showed her the little button. "You just press this if you need more."

"Dr. Sunny. I'll be fine. You give me a dose, and I'll take a wee rest before the service tonight."

I left her and nodded to the novice coming to take my place by her bedside.

Mother Superior was waiting for me in the parlor. I sat down and smiled at her.

"Success, Mother," I announced. "She's agreed to a little bit of morphine."

"You are a true miracle worker, child," Mother said with a smile. "Is there a catch?"

I laughed. "How did you know? Yes, there is a catch. She wants to attend the evening prayer service."

"We can manage that," she said. "You are looking well. I trust everything is going fine?"

I blushed. I always felt Mother Superior could look right into my inner soul. Did she know about Callum and me?

"I've been busy," I said, a bit evasively. "Last week, I had lunch with my mother and family."

I explained what happened in the orchard to the little girl. I didn't bring Callum into the conversation. Why muddy things?

"You find adventure everywhere, Dr. Sunny," she said. "Are you ready for dinner?"

"I'm always up for good food," I replied.

"You can join us in the dining room if you don't mind."

"Mind? I'm honored."

We walked down a long hallway and into the main dining area. A delicious aroma drifted from the adjacent kitchen, filling the dining area with warmth. Several novices were busy bringing dishes from the kitchen, and another laid the table with simple white plates and cutlery.

I walked over to the sink, washed my hands, and sat down next to Mother Superior. We waited until all the nuns and novices were seated.

Mother Superior asked, "Dr. Sunny, would you feel comfortable leading us in grace?"

I breathed in deeply and thought for a second before replying, "My mother always told me to imagine our fingers representing different religions, and just as the fingers come together on the wrist, all religions are united in the end with God. I'm not sure I know what to say."

The nun looked approvingly at me, "As usual, your mother has taught you well. Just give thanks to the Lord for the meal."

I nodded, bowed, and said, "Dear Lord, thank you for bringing us together for this delicious meal. We thank you for this bounty. We ask you to bless Sister Clarice and ease her suffering. Amen."

There was an echo of Amens, and one of the novices passed me bread and butter. There were bowls of vegetable soup, a simple green salad with lemon dressing, and melt-in-your-mouth lavender-infused cookies. We ate in silence, enjoying every bite. Mother Superior finally spoke only after we were served the cookies and hot herbal tea.

"Thanks to our doctor," she began. "Sister Clarice is resting comfortably. She wants to attend evening service with us, and I thought Mary Ruth and Sarah could set up a space for the sister's bed in the chapel."

I left them making plans and found Ragu waiting for me by the front gate.

"Ready, Dr. Sunny?" he asked.

"Yes, Ragu. I am. Sister Clarice is in good hands."

CHAPTER THIRTY-SEVEN
SUNNY AND THE VILLAGE SHAMAN
(A FEW WEEKS LATER)

I was still high from my picnic with Callum. I had enjoyed walking the entire perimeter of his estate. The views were spectacular, and I could easily see how this property could attract tourists and visitors. When we returned to the house, we found a picnic basket waiting for us on the green lawn. There was a container for fresh water and a piece of dried jerky for Karu. Callum opened the basket and laid out a thick blanket. We feasted on finger sandwiches, salad, fruit, and sparkling water. I felt extremely comfortable with him. We hadn't openly declared our feelings for each other, but I knew we shared something deep and meaningful. A few weeks later, I still smiled at the happy memory.

My euphoria disappeared quickly when I saw who was waiting for me. I remembered her from a previous visit. She was one of the village Shaman's "patients." His clients always ended up needing expensive and painful after-care.

That was the case with this patient, a young woman named Durga. A few weeks ago, she had come to see me with a broken arm, which had not been set correctly. The arm was healing in a grotesque position that was quite uncomfortable. The only way to help her was to break her arm again and re-cast it.

"What happened?" I remembered asking her. "Why didn't you come to me?"

The woman looked frightened and at first refused to answer my questions. When I explained what needed to be done, she started to cry. Her tears seemed to open up something inside her, and soon, she told me her story.

She lived in a village deep in the valley, quite far from the clinic. A friend drove her today. The Shaman was a despot and dictator. No one was allowed to go to the clinic or government hospital without his permission. The woman had fallen down off an embankment and broken her arm. Her family had taken her to the Shaman, who had insisted that the gods would heal her arm. The family offered flowers, fruits, grains, and money to the Shaman. Over the months, the arm had healed but was never the same again. When the pain had become unbearable, she had convinced her cousin to help her get to the clinic.

"I know when I go back, I will be punished for coming to see you," she had said, sobbing quietly, "But the pain was too much, and who is going to marry a cripple who can't milk a cow or carry firewood?"

I had made sure she got to the hospital. She had been admitted to the hospital where a surgeon re-set her arm. The last I heard; she had been staying at the hospital. Now she was back.

I greeted her and asked how she was doing.

"Dr. Sunny," she replied. "You were right about my arm. It is now healing well, and the doctor said I will have full use of my arm when the cast comes off."

She hesitated and looked at me with pleading eyes.

"I need your help, Dr. Sunny," she said. "I can't go back to the village by myself. Will you come with me? Please"

I sighed inwardly. "Of course, I can come with you, Durga."

Since there were no other patients, I asked Girija to keep an eye on the clinic and went to find Ragu, who was working in the living room installing a wood stove.

"Give me a few minutes to clean up, and we can go," he said when I told him about Durga.

Soon, Karu and I were bouncing along in the jeep to Durga's village.

"Tell me about the Shaman," I asked Durga.

Durga laughed, but it was a bitter sound.

"He is a priest and healer. He is known for driving out spirits from people who have been possessed. He doesn't believe in medicines or herbs. For that, the women consult Bhadra.

"The Shaman's family has been village priests for many decades. His grandfather, a long-time healer, was an honest man. But the current Shaman is not a good man. He is proud and believes he knows everything. He is called Murlisamy."

She paused. "He threatens us when we don't do as we are told. I'm frightened of him."

I wanted Durga to be safe and promised not to provoke the Shaman. My mother always said actions speak louder than words.

"If you do something, that is much better than just talking about it," she would say.

As I sat in the jeep wondering what I could do to help the situation, Ragu drove down a steep hill and stopped on the plateau. A group of people were standing around. I could hear the sounds of wailing and yelling. An older man was circling the crowd. He appeared to be performing some kind of bizarre dance, leaping about and waving his arms.

"Stay here, Dr. Sunny," Ragu said, getting out of the jeep.

Of course, I didn't listen to him. I was a doctor, and it was my job to help.

The villagers stepped aside, and I saw a young girl on the ground, crying quietly. The wailing woman didn't help the situation.

"Quiet," I said in a loud voice. "I'm a doctor. Let me help this girl."

"You are not touching this girl," yelled the man who had been leaping around.

I glared at him.

He paused and took a deep breath. "You know who I am? I am Murlisamy, and she is in my care. Doctor, your services are not needed here."

"Exactly what are you doing?" I asked.

We both looked down at the girl, and I could see a bone protruding from her broken ankle.

The Shaman replied, "I'm praying over her. My prayers will heal her and soon she will be able to walk."

I was about to push him aside and treat the girl, but one of the women did the job for me.

"Don't be foolish," she said in an angry voice. "The girl is not something to be experimented on. Move aside and let the doctor take care of her."

"She is my daughter," the Shaman said, waving the woman aside.

"She's my daughter, too," the woman insisted. "Do you remember what happened when that boy broke his arm? You healed him so well that now he can't move his arm. Or how about Durga and her broken arm?

At the mention of her name, Durga stepped forward and said in a timid voice, "Great mother," she addressed the woman respectfully, "Dr. Sunny healed me, and soon I will be able to move

~ 229 ~

my arm. You should let Dr. Sunny help Tara, or she will never walk again."

I added, "I can treat her so that she will not be a cripple."

"Did you hear that, Murlisamy?" the woman asked. She turned to me and said, "You go ahead and help my Tara."

I nodded and squatted beside the girl.

"Tara, my name is Dr. Sunny, and I will help you."

I looked around for Ragu.

"Ragu," I shouted out. "I need your help. Get some bandages from my medical bag."

I turned to the girl's mother. "I need something to stabilize her ankle. Can you find two pieces of wood as flat and straight about two feet long?" I said, using my hands to show the length of the wood.

The woman nodded and walked away. Just as Ragu brought me the bandages and my bag, the woman returned with several pieces of wood. I chose a couple and set to work.

"We are going to make a splint to keep the ankle as immobile as possible," I said. "I can't do anything else right now."

I used the wood to hold her ankle in place and wrapped it snuggly with the bandages.

I was about to offer Tara some pain pills only to discover the girl had fainted from the pain and trauma. There was nothing more I could do for her right now. I stood up and wiped my hands on my jeans.

"Alright, now we need to get her to the hospital," I said. I looked at the Shaman and asked, "Will you come with us?"

He turned his back to me.

"I'll come with you," the mother said.

"Durga, can you find your way back home?" I asked.

"I'll be fine, Dr. Sunny," she said with a smile. "You have done what you set out to do."

It took a moment for me to realize she was right.

I smiled and patted her on the shoulder. "Yes, I made my point. Come see me in two weeks so we can remove the cast. I will also show you some exercises to strengthen your arm."

It was late at night when Ragu and I returned home. Tara's break had required surgery, but now she was resting at the hospital. I was glad I had saved her from becoming a cripple. She would walk again after some intensive physical therapy.

CHAPTER THIRTY-EIGHT
CALLUM'S UNEXPECTED VISITOR

The picnic and hike around his property cemented his feeling for Sunny. Once his business was up and running, he would talk to Little Mother and Raj and propose to Sunny. He decided he wanted to spend the rest of his life with her.

He was still thinking about Sunny and was shocked to see Ella standing at the front door.

"Hello, darling. Surprise!" she said lightly as she stood on tiptoe to kiss his cheek.

"Ella, what are you doing here?" he managed to ask.

"I heard from your mom you were homesick and missing everyone. I thought, why not go to India and bring a bit of Scotland to Callum."

"Why didn't you let me know?"

"Then, it wouldn't be a surprise, silly. Aren't you glad to see me?"

"I'm surprised for sure," he said, a little exasperated. "Where are my manners? Come in. What are your plans?"

"This is my first stop. I'm on my way to visit a friend in New Delhi. You left in a hurry, and we never had a chance to talk."

He led her into the living room. Shanta had started a fire, and the place was warm and cozy.

"This is lovely," she said, sitting on the sofa. "Come sit by me and tell me what you've been doing. Your mom sounded so mysterious when I last talked to her."

"Ella, I'd love to catch up with you, but I'm late for a meeting. I'll let my housekeeper know you are here. She'll fix you some breakfast and get you settled. We can talk when I get back."

He escaped before she could say anything. Shanta was in the kitchen.

"Are you ready for breakfast, Scot Sir," she asked.

He replied, "Actually, Shanta, I have an unexpected guest. Can you fix her breakfast and settle her in the spare room?'

"Her? Who is here? Dr. Sunny?"

He shook his head. "I wish," he ran his fingers through his hair, an old habit when he was frustrated, and said, "No, it's an old friend from Scotland. Her name is Ella, and can you keep her entertained today?"

"Oh, like that, is it? I can feed her breakfast. I'm not a babysitter. I'm going to the village this afternoon to see a man about getting some fresh buffalo milk delivered. She is on her own."

Callum was taken aback by her reply but didn't argue.

"That will be fine. I'll be back for dinner. I'm meeting Raj and then heading to a meeting with his father and another investor in Upper Mahagiri."

"What about your tea and breakfast?"

"I'll stop at the Woodlands Hotel. Give my breakfast to Ella," he said.

He couldn't get out of the house fast enough. Shanta shook her head. She was curious to meet this old friend from Scotland.

CHAPTER THIRTY-NINE
SUNNY'S UNPLEASANT SURPRISE

I hadn't seen Callum for the past few days because I had been so busy. Even though we talked on the phone daily, I missed seeing him. We closed the clinic on Tuesday afternoon so Ragu could finish the last bit of plumbing in the exam room. I decided this was the perfect opportunity to take Karu for a walk. What if the hike took me down a hill, across a canyon, up another hill, and past Callum's house? I imagined his surprised look and grinned to myself.

"Come on, Karu, let's go," I said. "Girija, I'll be back in a couple of hours. I have my cell phone."

I filled the canteen with water and headed out the door with Karu. It was a cool day with a stiff breeze. Karu was happy to run ahead, following the scents on the hillside. When we reached the top of the hill, I stopped to look at the view of the valley below me. I could see the clinic in the distance. I took a sip of water. I filled my palm with water and let Karu drink some of the liquid. She made a slimy mess. I wiped my hands on my pants and started up the embankment toward Callum's estate.

I wanted to surprise him, so I decided to use the front door. In the past, I usually entered through the side kitchen gate. I tied Karu to a small bush. She plopped down on the cool grass. I patted her head and walked up the steps. I rapped on the wooden door and waited. When nothing happened, I raised my hand to knock again when the door swung open to reveal a woman in the doorway. She wore one of Callum's shirts, which hung just above her bare knees. Her feet were bare, and she had a towel wrapped around her head. She looked like she just stepped out of the bath.

"Oh," she said. "Are you looking for the housekeeper? Shanta? I think she's in the kitchen."

For a moment, I couldn't find my voice. I cleared my throat.

"Okay," I said, my voice sounding squeaky to me. "Are you visiting?"

She smiled brightly at me. "Well, yes, I am. I'm Callum's girlfriend from Scotland. I just popped in for a visit."

She made it as if to close the door. "It's getting a little chilly here. I better get dressed before Callum comes back. He left rather early this morning."

I blinked, feeling a bit stupid. I stepped back, nearly stumbling in my haste to leave.

"Wait," she yelled. "I didn't get your name."

I didn't reply. I ran around to the side where Karu was waiting for me. I lay down next to the dog, hiding my face in my folded arms. Karu nuzzled my neck with a wet nose. I could still hear her musical accent, similar to Callum's. *I'm Callum's girlfriend from Scotland.*

Callum had made a fool of me! I had believed his claims he didn't have a girlfriend. Why would he lie to me? My thoughts were in a jumble. I didn't know how long I lay there, but I knew it was time to go home. I didn't want Shanta to find me on the grass. Obviously, I had no business being here on this property. Everything had been a lie. He was using me to get close to my family. It had been all about his business. Whatever the reason, it was time for this charade to end. I sat up, blinking in the sunlight. Like that man in the fairy tale, I felt like I had been sleeping for a long time. Rip Van Winkle, waking up from a long nap. Perhaps I was still asleep, and this whole thing was a bad nightmare. The pup sat up, eager to move.

"Come on, Karu, let's go home," my voice was weary.

My heart was breaking with each step I took toward the clinic. Stupid, foolish girl, I whispered to myself. I don't remember the walk home, but I asked Girija for a hot bath as soon as I got there.

"Are you okay? You don't look well, Dr. Sunny," she said.

I wanted to tell her I was suffering from a broken heart, one that couldn't be fixed by a doctor. I shook my head and said, "I'm tired. I need an early night. Can you feed Karu?"

"Of course, Dr. Sunny," she said.

I poured hot water over my body, wishing memories could be washed away like sandalwood soap suds. I slipped into my oldest and comfiest sweats and shirt and climbed into bed. Girija, bless her heart, had left a tray of soup, bread, and cake. I took a few sips of the soup, which was hot and nourishing, even though I had no appetite. The bread tasted like a thick dust rag, and I couldn't bear to eat the sweet cake. I put the tray on the table beside my bed and drank some water before climbing under the sheets. Of course, I couldn't sleep. I lay still and pretended to be asleep. Maybe I could fool my body and mind.

CHAPTER FORTY

SUNNY'S HEARTACHE

I woke up the next day bleary-eyed and heavy-limbed. I was sick, but it wasn't my body that was ailing; it was my very soul. Girija came in to check on me.

"You don't have a fever," she said, using the time-tested method of taking a person's temperature. Her fingers were cool on my forehead. "But you don't look good. Let me make you some kangee."

I wanted to sit up and say, "I'm fine. It's just a broken heart. I can see patients today."

But I was unable to speak. Girija left with a worried look on her face. She came back with a bowl of kangee. Kangee is India's remedy for everything from colds to upset stomachs. White rice is cooked until it is soft and pliable. Then, it is hand squeezed, preferably by your mother, until it is broken down and forms a thick soup. This soupy rice was flavored with plenty of sea salt. Sometimes a bit of ghee is added, or a knob of fresh butter. Some cooks add chopped and cooked greens. Others add a bit of fresh cilantro leaves. Some like to serve it with yogurt or a bit of ripe banana. Girija had opted for ghee and slivers of raw onion. I managed to eat a few mouthfuls. I knew I had to get up. I had responsibilities.

"Dr. Sunny," Girija's voice was timid. "There is a patient here who needs your help. He looks pretty bad."

Just like that, my broken heart was forgotten. I dressed in seconds and was out in the exam room. The man was dehydrated, and I started him on an IV and gave him something to settle his stomach. The poor man had a severe case of the stomach flu.

"Once you feel better, I want you to go home and have some ginger tea with honey," I instructed him,

"You aren't giving me any medicines?" he asked.

That was the trouble; everyone wanted pills and potions when ginger tea was just as effective with no side effects. I had Girija bring me a cup of hot ginger tea and after drinking it he left, looking much better. I was starting to feel better, too.

The morning passed quickly as I saw patients, updated charts, and had a light lunch of broth, steamed veggies, and fresh fruit.

"How are you feeling, Dr. Sunny?" Girija asked as she gathered the dirty dishes. "Doctors need to take care of themselves too."

I smiled at her concern and replied, "I feel much better now. You have taken good care of me."

"Exactly what happened?" she asked in a curious voice.

"I think it might have been too much sun, and along with exhaustion I was just feeling drained."

This was a white lie, I thought to myself.

She nodded and looked like she wanted to say something. I waited, but she left without saying a word.

When the last patient left, I closed the clinic, whistled for Karu, and set off for the mission. A talk with the Mother Superior was in order.

"Girija, please send Ragu to pick me up from the mission just after dark," I said.

Was it just yesterday that Karu and I had been hiking to Callum's house? I shook my head; I didn't want to think about him. I couldn't bear to deal with my emotions.

It felt good to move around and be outside in the fresh air. The dog was happy to sniff and run ahead of me. I followed her and before I knew it, I was at the mission gates. As usual, the gates were open and welcoming. I wondered what I was going to say to the Mother Superior. I wanted her advice, but this was a delicate subject. Was love and betrayal something to discuss with a nun? Perhaps I should just turn around and leave.

"Dr. Sunny, what are you doing here? I hope there is no emergency?"

It was a novice named Sister Ruth.

I waved and walked toward her. "No, no. I was just out walking my dog, "I said. "My feet seem to have brought me to the mission."

I laughed a little nervously.

The novice nodded with a serious expression and said, "Yes, sometimes our body knows what the soul craves. Come in, and I'll see if Mother is free."

She stopped and looked down at the dog. "Karu, come with me."

My dog followed her happily, hoping for a treat or two.

I walked down through the herb garden, which was fragrant and peaceful. I could hear the buzzing of the bees. No one was working in the garden, and I had the place to myself. I sat on the stone bench, closed my eyes, and let the peace and quiet enter my body. A kind of sitting yoga. I breathed in deeply. Lavender, honeysuckle, and other scents floated into my nostrils. It was soothing and serene.

"Ah, there you are, Doctor Sunny," Mother Superior said as she approached the path. "Ruth just told me that you were here."

She sat beside me and said, "It is lovely here, isn't it? So peaceful one can feel God's powerful presence here."

She sighed and looked at me. I kept my head down.

"What brings you here on a Tuesday afternoon? No patients?"

I shook my head and answered, "No, it was quiet, so I took Karu for a walk and found myself at your gates."

The nun laughed softly. "It is said the mission draws people in. But I thought your walks took you up the hill to Dorai Raj's old place these days?"

I was a little startled by her question and turned my head to look at her.

"Why are you surprised?" she asked. "Dear child, this is a small place, and everyone knows everyone else's business."

I wanted to ask her if she knew about Callum's visitor, but instead, I said, "I'm not sure that walk is right for me anymore."

The nun didn't say anything for a moment. "You came to see me, Dr. Sunny, so tell me what's on your mind."

Mother Superior had always been outspoken, something I liked about her.

I sighed and sat up straighter before replying, "I don't know if you are aware, but I've been seeing a lot of Callum."

Her blue eyes twinkled, and she said, "Oh, child, as I said, this is a small village, remember?"

I blushed. I was mortified that someone was always watching me and my movements. I should have known. This had frustrated Meena and was one of the reasons she had left Mahagiri for California. I had stayed out of the limelight because, as the younger daughter, I was not as visible, and my actions didn't warrant the attention of the entire village.

"I should have known," I said a little bitterly. "Then you know why I'm here."

"Oh, dear one, I don't know why you are here. As I said, you and Callum have been seen at the Country Club dining room. That is the rumor I heard, and I was happy for both of you."

I looked at her and asked, "You don't think it was a mistake?"

"A mistake? Why do you say that? Sunny, only you know your heart."

"It's not that simple," I said, twisting my hands. "I wish I knew what to do."

"Why don't you tell me what is happening, and perhaps I can help. And in any case, talking about it might make you feel better."

I slowly told her about visiting Callum, finding Ella wearing his shirt, and waiting for him to come home. She had called herself his girlfriend.

I swallowed a lump in my throat as I remembered the scene at the front door.

My voice echoed my disappointment. "He specifically told me he didn't have a girlfriend, and I believed him."

The nun asked in a gentle voice, "Have you spoken to Callum about this visitor?"

I shook my head in surprise.

"Then you are talking to the wrong person, Dr. Sunny. You should be asking Callum."

She added, "Do you trust him?"

I thought for a long moment.

"Yes," I finally said. "I like him and trust him. In fact, maybe I more than like him."

"Well, then, Dr. Sunny, you have to talk to Callum in person. Sometimes, we let our imagination run wild. Looks like a heart-to-heart is just what you need."

I laughed, suddenly feeling lighter. "Thank you, Mother Superior," I said. "I'll do that."

I paused momentarily and said, "I'm sorry to hear of Sister Clarice's passing."

The nun sighed and said, "Life would not be life without death. Sister Clarice is with the Lord and is no longer in pain."

I touched her hand and said, "Still, it is difficult to lose someone."

"And our order keeps shrinking," the nun said. "But those are worries for another day. When is Ragu coming to pick you up?"

I replied, "I should call him."

"Go on then, use the telephone, get home, and make your plans."

She added, "Come back and tell me how the story ends."

Soon, Ragu, Karu, and I were in the jeep heading home. I waited until the couple had gone to bed before going to the exam room to use the telephone. I dialed Callum's number and waited as it rang and rang. No one was home.

I had looked forward to talking to him and felt let down. I sighed as I returned to bed, where I spent most of the night staring at the ceiling.

The following day, I tried calling Callum again. This time, the phone was picked up right away. It was a woman who answered.

"Ella speaking," I heard her saying.

I hung up and stared at the receiver as if it was a poisonous snake. All my doubts came rushing back. Luckily, I had patients waiting to distract me.

Around mid-morning, I was taking a quick tea break when I heard a car pulling up in front of the clinic. Another patient?

I hurried outside and came to an abrupt stop on the top step. It was Callum. I watched him get out and walk toward the clinic. He stopped at the bottom of the porch steps.

"Sunny," he started to say.

CHAPTER FORTY-ONE
CALLUM'S DILEMMA

He was suddenly tongue-tied at the sight of Sunny standing on the clinic porch, especially because she looked like an avenging angel.

He had come home late last night in hopes of avoiding Ella. But no such luck. She was waiting for him to tell him about the visitor. She had giggled as she recounted the look on the native woman's face.

"She looked so shocked to see me in your shirt," Ella said with a laugh. "I didn't realize Indians were so modest."

He had wanted to strangle her. He wanted to call Sunny right away, but it was nearly midnight. As soon as the sun rose, he drove over to the clinic. Now, he was face-to-face with his dream and nightmare.

"Sunny," he said, walking toward the porch.

"Dr. Sunny," Girija shouted as she ran out of the house. "You have a phone call. Your sister is in trouble."

Without a word, Sunny turned around and rushed back into the house.

Girija looked at him and said loudly, "You should go. The doctor is busy."

He needed to talk to her, so he waited. Sunny rushed out of the house and paused briefly when she saw him.

"Sunny, can I help? I can drive you."

She shook her head, distracted. "No, no. Ragu is taking me."

He watched her walk toward the waiting jeep. He turned and walked back into the clinic. Girija was clearing the dining room table, and she looked up at him.

"Girija, I need to talk to her," he pleaded. "Please tell me what is going on. Where is Dr. Sunny rushing off to?"

The woman shook her head and went about clearing the table. She glanced at him, and when she saw his anguished face, she relented and spoke to him.

"Alright," she said. "She's gone to the government hospital. Her sister is having a baby. Don't you dare distract…."

He didn't wait for her to finish her sentence because he was already running to his jeep. Within a few seconds he on his to Lower Mahagiri.

CHAPTER FORTY-TWO

SUNNY AND MEENA

My mother's brief phone call did not have a lot of details. She said she was on the way to the hospital with Meena. Ragu drove fast, but inwardly, I kept urging him to go faster.

The road and hillsides were obscured by a light mist swirling around us. The late morning fog could be dense and deadly, and perhaps driving fast wasn't a good idea. Just as I was about to ask Ragu to slow down, he brought the jeep to a screeching halt. It looked like he had just stopped before hitting something on the road.

I grabbed the door handle and struggled to open the jeep door.

"What is it?" I yelled out to him.

He didn't reply. Instead, he jumped out of the vehicle. I followed him just in time to see him help someone up. Who was it?

I was shocked when I saw Bhadra try to stand up.

"Bhadra? What is going on?" I asked as I supported her. "Are you hurt?"

She shook her head to indicate she was alright but gratefully leaned on me as we walked back to the jeep.

"I'm fine, Dr. Sunny. I was on my way to see you. I was crossing the road when I saw the jeep's headlights. I knew it was you and rushed to stop you. It's your family that needs help."

I stared at the woman. "What do you mean?"

She winced as she climbed into the back seat and spoke to Ragu.

"Ragu, go on and drive. We need to get to the hospital as soon as possible."

I turned around to look at the medicine woman. "How did you know where we were going?"

She smiled at me. "Dr. Sunny, is that the question you want to ask me?"

I laughed nervously. "No, no. Bhadra, what do you mean someone in my family needs help?"

She sighed. "I had a vision about your sister."

"Meena?"

"Yes, she was in a lot of pain, and the baby was in distress."

I looked at the woman huddled in the back seat and chewed on my lip, a nervous habit.

"Did you see anything else? Will she be all right? Will the baby be alright?"

"Dr. Sunny, that's not how a vision works. I just know I have to be there to help her."

We drove in silence, and after a long time (or so it seemed to me), we finally arrived at Lower Mahagiri. Ragu drove down the main road, past the shops, and to the government hospital. He had barely stopped when I leaped out of the car. I opened the back seat and helped Bhadra out. I almost dragged the poor woman with me to the hospital entrance. After a few hectic moments of explanation, we were directed to a wing of the vast hospital. I found my mother waiting in the corridor.

"Amma," I hugged her tightly and asked. "What is going on?"

She wiped her eyes on her sari and looked at me her eyes shining with unshed tears, "Your sister was complaining of back pain. I didn't think it was labor pains, so I massaged her back, and Devi gave her a warm bath. Nothing helped. Then she started to spot, and I had Jaibal drive us here. A doctor is examining her now."

She used her head to indicate the room behind us. I nodded and touched her shoulder before knocking on the closed door. I entered and found my sister on the bed, looking pale and worried.

"Sunny," she said. "You came."

"Of course, I did, silly," I said, kneeling by her bed.

The doctor looked up and frowned.

"This is my sister, Sunny," Meena said. "She's a doctor."

The doctor nodded and said, "Ah, I've heard of you, Dr. Sunny. I'm Dr. Parvathi."

She stripped off her gloves. Her eyes were grave behind thick spectacles.

I gripped Meena's hand, waiting for good news.

Dr. Parvathi addressed Meena, "First of all, your baby's heartbeat is strong, which is a good sign. Your bleeding has stopped for now, so I think the best thing to do is for you to stay so that we can monitor you."

The doctor left the room. I kissed Meena's forehead.

"Meena, I'll go get Ma," I said.

I ran down the hallway and caught up with the doctor.

"Doctor Parvathi," I called out. "Please, can I have a moment of your time?"

The woman turned and stared at me with a questioning look.

"I'm sorry to bother you," I said. "I thought bleeding in late pregnancy meant emergency C-section."

She nodded and said, "Normally, if the baby is distressed or the mother is unhealthy. But your sister is extremely healthy, and the baby's heartbeat seems strong. I prefer to wait a few hours and see how things progress."

I agreed and thanked her. I was about to walk away when Bhadra joined us.

She reached out and clutched the doctor's hand, looking a little crazy, "Doctor, you have to operate right now," she said. "The baby is in danger."

The doctor recoiled from Bhadra. "What? Who are you?" she demanded.

"I'm Bhadra from the village of Kalarajanad. This morning, I had a vision of Meena and her baby. The baby was struggling in the womb, wanting to come out, but something was preventing the birth. The baby is in terrible distress. I know this."

The doctor shook her head and tried to move away. "Listen, I'm used to village women and their superstitions," she said firmly. "This is crazy old-fashioned talk and doesn't belong in a modern hospital. Someone needs to remove this woman at once."

She looked around for help. I stood still, my eyes darting between Bhadra and the doctor. Then, I knew what I had to do.

I walked up to the doctor and placed my hand on her arm in what I hoped was a reassuring manner.

"Doctor Parvathi, I know this sounds outlandish and strange," I said in a low voice. "I know this woman. She is not crazy. Can you please go back and check on my sister? Please."

The doctor looked at me and then at Bhadra as if trying to see who was crazier. Finally, she nodded, and I let out a breath I didn't know I was holding.

Dr. Parvathi entered my sister's room with both of us right behind her. It was a peaceful scene, and I felt a momentary twinge of doubt. My mother sat next to my sister, who had her eyes closed. The baby monitor was sending out a steady rhythm. Everything looked normal.

"See," the doctor looked at us with accusing eyes and said, "It's all okay in here. Now, I have other patients."

She turned to leave, but Bhadra stepped in front of her. I watched, wide-eyed, as Bhadra drew herself up straight and tossed her head. Her curly hair swirled forming a bizarre halo around her. Even the doctor seemed mesmerized by all that moving hair. We all just stared.

"Doctor," Bhadra's voice was loud and commanding. "Check the machine. I'm telling you that the baby is in danger."

Bhadra's demeanor was alarming everyone, including my sister, who tried to sit up. My mother stepped up and, as usual, took charge.

"Doctor Parvathi, is it?" she spoke in a soothing voice. "I'm sorry you are caught up in the middle. But this is my daughter and grandchild here. Can you please just take another look?"

The doctor didn't do anything for a whole minute, and then she moved to check on Meena, but Bhadra grabbed her arm.

"Stop," she almost shouted. We were all startled, and the doctor was starting to look very annoyed. "Check the machine."

"What?" the doctor sounded confused and annoyed. "What are you saying?"

Bhadra shook her head. "You said the heartbeat sounded healthy," she shouted. "But I know something is wrong, so it must be the machine."

I pushed past the doctor and Bhadra and knelt down by the wall. I wiggled the plug of the fetal monitor. There was a long pause, and the machine started to beep furiously.

The doctor sprang into action.

"Everyone out," she yelled. "Nurse, get these people out and help me."

I didn't wait to hear what else she said as I was ushered out with my mother and Bhadra.

Once in the hallway, I hugged my friend and asked her, "How did you know?"

She shook her head and replied simply, "The Goddess spoke to me."

My mother looked worried as she said, "I hope everything will be alright."

Bhadra hugged my mother before replying, "It will, Little Mother. Lord Yama is not coming today."

While we were waiting, Raj rushed down the hallway.

"Amma, Sunny," he was out of breath. "What happened? I just got the message that Meena was here."

My mother stood up to tell him what was going on. Raj sat down next to me, a dazed expression on his face. The door to Meena's room opened, and I saw a gurney come out, pushed by an orderly.

Raj stood up and walked up to the doctor.

"Are you the father?" she asked. He nodded. "Well, we are taking your wife for an emergency C-Section. You are welcome to come with us. Follow the nurse to get your gown and slippers."

With a nod at us and an unreadable look at Bhadra, Dr. Parvathi continued down the hall. I let out a deep sigh.

"Oh, Amma," I said.

"I know, *kutty*," she replied. "Is that Callum?"

I turned my head to see Callum coming down the hall. I stood up.

"I have to go to the bathroom," I said as I took off in the opposite direction.

Mother Superior's advice had been sound, and I knew I had to talk to Callum, but I couldn't bear to do it right now.

I stayed in the overheated restroom for a long time. The door finally swung open, and Bhadra came in.

"He's gone, Dr. Sunny," she said. Her eyes flashed sympathy and something else. Was it amusement? "It's safe for you to come out."

I didn't reply. I walked out and sat back down on the bench. A few minutes later, my mother joined us. Neither of us said anything. It seemed like a long wait. We all jumped up when Raj came running down the hallway.

"It's a boy," he said, a wide grin splitting his face. He was still dressed in a hospital gown and cap. We drew together for a group hug.

"When can we see her?" my mother asked.

"Soon," Raj said. "They are taking her to recovery. We can go and wait for her there."

As we made our way to the recovery wing, I squeezed Bhadra's hand.

"Thank you," I whispered.

"Everything is in the Goddess's hands," she whispered back. "We are but ants in this universe."

CHAPTER FORTY-THREE
CALLUM'S MISTAKE

Watching Sunny run into the restroom to avoid speaking to him was heart-wrenching. He stood still, wondering what to do, when he felt a tap on his shoulder. Little Mother was standing next to him.

"Little Mother," he said. "I didn't mean to intrude on a private family moment."

She smiled and said, "You didn't intrude. What is going on, Callum? You and Sunny were best friends one moment, and now she runs away from you."

He ran his hand through his hair and replied, "I'm sorry, Little Mother, but I may have made a mistake."

"A mistake?"

Her voice was sharp, and he took a deep breath.

"Actually, it was a misunderstanding. Your daughter thought she saw something but it wasn't what she thought she saw."

"You aren't making any sense, Callum," Little Mother said. "Come, let's walk, and you can try explaining it to me."

He told her about finding Ella on his doorstep and how Sunny had met her and had assumed Ella was still his girlfriend.

"She no longer means anything to me," he said. "But I can't get Sunny to listen."

The older woman stopped and gazed at him with sharp eyes.

"Callum, what are your intentions toward my daughter?"

"Little Mother, I'm now confused about what to do. But my feelings for your daughter are clear. I love her."

"Does she feel the same about you?"

"I thought so," he admitted.

Little Mother stared into Callum's sad and devasted eyes.

"Are you serious about winning back my daughter's confidence?"

"Yes, more than anything else in the world."

The woman nodded and said, "Good, then you must find a way."

"But she's not talking to me," he said.

"So, you are giving up, then?"

He thought for a moment.

"No, I'm not, but I don't know how to break the ice to explain," he said, sounding frustrated.

"Then you need to think creatively, outside the box as they say."

There was silence as both of them pondered.

"I have an idea," Little Mother finally said. "You need help from the villagers."

"The villagers?"

"She loves her patients, and if you have their support, perhaps Sunny will listen to you."

He listened as Little Mother laid out a plan. It made sense, and Sunny would see that he was sincere if the villagers including Girija and Ragu supported him.

"That's a great idea, Little Mother," he said. "I know just the person I need to talk to."

He bent down and hugged the startled woman before taking off. He couldn't wait to go to the clinic and talk to Girija.

CHAPTER FORTY-FOUR
GIRIJA'S TROUBLES

Girija found herself humming as she picked through the rice. It was nice to be outside, enjoying the mild weather. She hoped Sunny's sister was doing all right. She wanted to call the hospital to find out but decided to wait for Ragu to come home.

She kept herself busy with cleaning, dusting, and preparing a meal. For the first time in her life, she was content and happy. Working at the clinic and caring for the doctor had given her life a new purpose. Ragu was a wonderfully supportive husband; memories of her abusive past were a distant memory.

She heard the dog barking in the living room, and suddenly, there was the sound of a yelp and then nothing.

"Karu!" she yelled as she ran from the kitchen.

She found the dog lying in the open doorway of the clinic. She feared the worst as she knelt down to check on the animal. She heard a noise and looked up into the wild eyes of a man standing in the clinic. He was holding a large, curved knife used to cut open coconuts.

For a long moment, they stared at each other. Girija could feel her heart racing as she stood up. Her only thought was to get away from the man and his knife. Girija turned to run but the man grabbed her hair bun. The pain was excruciating, and she yelped in terror.

"Don't be stupid," he warned her. "Or you'll end up like this dog. Tell me, where's the medicine?"

She could smell toddy on his hot breath.

"I have no idea what you are talking about," she said.

He yanked her hair harder, and she screamed.

"The medicine the doctor gives out for pain. Where does she keep it?"

She started to say she didn't know but she didn't want her hair pulled again.

"It's in the clinic," she managed to gasp.

He turned her around, still holding tight to her hair.

"Show me," he said, pushing her forward.

"Here, it's here," she said as he pushed again. She had to step over the prone body of the dog to enter the room.

"That cupboard by the wall," she said, pointing to the locked cabinet.

He finally let go of her hair and shoved her to the floor. He walked over to the cupboard and yanked on the lock.

"Key?" he growled.

"I don't have the key," she said, flinching at the wild look in his eye.

He hauled her up by an arm and held the curved blade around her neck.

"Tell me where the key is, or I will slash your throat," he said, pressing the blade into her exposed neck.

She tried to shake her head, but he tightened his grip on her arm and pressed the blade so hard she could feel the sharp blade pierce her skin. Warm drops of blood dripped down her neck.

"I don't have it," she said. "The doctor takes it with her."

"You are worthless," he said. "I should just kill you now."

"Wait," she said. "Maybe it's in the drawer. Sometimes, she leaves it behind."

He removed the knife from her neck and motioned with it.

"Go on, where is it?"

She pretended to look and took out the key for the front door.

"Here it is," she said, holding out the key.

Her eyes widened when she saw Callum standing behind the man with a shovel. The man noticed her expression and started to turn around, but Callum was quicker and hit the man on the back of his head with the shovel. The man fell down without a sound.

Girija started to sob and rushed to Callum, who gathered her in his arms.

"It's alright, Girija," he said in a soothing voice. "It's all right. He can't hurt you now."

She sobbed into his chest and then pulled away.

"Karu," she said. "He has hurt Karu."

They both rushed to the living room, where the dog was still lying on the ground. Callum checked to see if the dog was breathing.

"Alright, she's alive," he said, relief clear in his voice, "But we need to take her to the vet right now."

"What about him?" Girija asked, gesturing toward the intruder.

"I'll take care of him," Callum said. "You wait in the jeep with Karu. I won't be long."

He carried the dog to his jeep, and Girija climbed in the back. He carefully placed the unconscious dog on the seat, and Girija cradled the Karu's head on her lap.

Callum ran back to the clinic and came out dragging the unconscious man by his arms to the old tree in front of the clinic, where he propped him up against the tree trunk. Callum returned to the house and came out with a long coil of rope, which he used to tie the man securely to the tree trunk.

"That should keep him until the authorities get here," he said as he entered the jeep.

"Did you call the police?" Girija asked.

"Yes," he nodded. "They are sending someone, but we can't wait for them. Let's get Karu to the animal clinic in Lower Mahagiri."

As he took off, he looked at Girija in his rearview mirror.

"Are you hurt?"

"No, I'm alright," she said.

"Your neck is bleeding," he said.

She wiped the blood off with the end of her sari.

"I'm alright," she said again.

The vet lived in a small house at the back of the clinic. Since it was after-hours, he went to the back door and banged on it.

"Coming, coming," a voice called from behind the closed door. "Keep your trousers on."

The door was opened by a young woman wearing thick black spectacles.

"Yes?"

"I have a dog that has been seriously hurt," Callum said.

He didn't get to say anything more because the vet pushed him aside and rushed to the clinic to unlock the doors.

"Well, don't just stand there," she yelled. "Bring the dog inside."

Soon, Karu was on the exam table.

"What happened?" she demanded as she began her examination.

The vet looked at them, but it was Girija who answered, "She was hurt by a thief looking for drugs," she said, her voice trembling slightly. "I think he kicked her when she tried to stop him."

The vet's severe expression relaxed a bit.

"There's a tea stall down the street," she said. "Go, get a cup, and I'll take care of…."

"Karu, her name is Karu," Callum said.

He then led Girija to the waiting room.

"You wait here," he said. "I'll get us a cup of tea."

"No," Girija clutched his arm. "Don't leave me alone."

"I won't be but a moment," Callum said gently.

But Girija shook her head.

"I don't need tea," she said.

"Alright, we'll wait together."

They waited in silence, with Girija still holding onto Callum's arm.

Finally, the vet came out of the exam room.

"I've examined Karu. She has a bruised rib, and she banged her head pretty badly, which is why she is unconscious. I've bandaged her up and given her something for the pain, but she needs to be monitored for the next twenty-four hours."

"I can do that," Callum said, standing up.

"No," the vet shook her head. "You take the lady and get her injuries examined, and I'll keep Karu overnight. I'll take good care of her. You can come pick her up tomorrow morning. Are you the owner?" she asked.

Callum shook his head and replied, "No, that would be Dr. Sunny."

"Oh, I know, Dr. Sunny," the vet smiled. "Tell her to come tomorrow."

"Thank you," Callum said.

"Come on, Girija," he said. "Let's get you to the hospital."

Even though Girija insisted she was okay, he drove her to the government hospital. As they pulled into the parking lot, they saw Ragu walking to the jeep.

"Ragu," Callum called out.

The man came over. "Sir? What's going on?"

He peered into the car and saw Girija. He ran around the front of the car and opened the passenger side door.

"Girija, oh my God," he cried out. "What happened? You are bleeding."

The next few minutes were a jumble of words and explanations, but finally, the entire story spilled out of Girija.

"Where's Sunny?" Callum asked.

"She has gone home with Raj," Ragu said. "I, too, was on my way home when you called out my name."

"I guess I'll head back to the clinic and see what has happened with the thief," Callum said, returning to his jeep. "Ragu, make sure you get Girija looked at."

"Wait," Girija said. She ran up to him and wrapped her arms around him. "Thank you for saving my life. I'll never forget it."

"Yes, thank you, sir," Ragu said, shaking Callum's hand. "I'll make sure Girija sees a doctor."

CHAPTER FORTY-FIVE

SHANTA TAKES OVER

It was dark when Callum arrived at the clinic, and every-thing was quiet. He noticed a policeman standing in front of the building and stopped the jeep.

"Is the thief in custody?" he asked the policeman.

The man nodded as he came up to the jeep.

"Yes, sir," he said. "He is now in jail. I'm guarding the clinic until the owners return."

Callum thanked the officer and drove up the hill to his estate. He found Shanta waiting for him.

"There you are, Scot Sir," she said, getting up from the living room chair. "You have been gone a while. You missed your friend Ella. She left this afternoon in a hurry. What did you say to her last night before you ran off to see Dr. Sunny?"

Callum looked at Shanta. "Nothing much. I just made it clear that Dr. Sunny was my priority now."

"Well, that is a good attitude," Shanta said. "How do you plan to win back the doctor?"

"I don't know," Callum admitted. "It has been a long day. Right now, I just want a hot bath and some dinner."

"You sit down. Have a snifter of your favorite drink, and I'll fill the tub," Shanta said. "I heard about what happened at the clinic. You were very courageous."

"Not really. It was Girija who was brave."

She poured him a generous serving of whiskey. He sighed as he sat down and accepted the drink. Callum took a sip and felt the warmth of the liquor relax him.

A little later, he was sitting in a tub of hot water, almost dozing off, when he heard Shanta knocking on the door.

"Scot Sir," she called out. "Don't fall asleep in the tub. I have dinner ready for you."

He entered the dining room to find a covered tray on the table. He sat down and removed the cover to find a bowl of spicy lentil soup. He took a sip.

Shanta came and stood by his side.

"So, what's the plan? I feel like I'm digging out a rotten tooth," she complained. "Getting you to talk is hard."

Callum finished the last of the soup and wiped his chin with the cloth napkin.

"Well, I talked to Little Mother at the hospital, and she had a strange suggestion," he said. "She wanted me to ask the villagers to help me win back Sunny."

Shanta stared at Callum for a long moment and then smiled broadly.

"That is a perfect suggestion," she said. "You get some rest. I have some work to do."

The alcohol, warm bath, and hot soup relaxed him, and Callum soon fell asleep, too tired to think of any plans. His last thought was of Sunny.

CHAPTER FORTY-SIX
SUNNY GETS SOME BAD NEWS

I felt like I had just lived a lifetime in the past few days. I was glad Meena was out of danger, and I had a brand-new nephew, but as Raj drove us to my mother's home, I could feel the exhaustion taking over my limbs and mind. I just wanted to sleep and forget the trauma of the past couple of days. The image of Callum was etched on the back of my eyelids. I rubbed them, hoping to erase the image.

Devi and Bindita were waiting for us at the front door, eager for news about Meena. It was late, and I was glad when we all went to bed. I had difficulty falling asleep even though I could feel the fatigue coursing through my limbs. I finally drifted off, only to be awakened by Devi.

"*Kutty*," she whispered urgently. "Wake up. You have a telephone call."

I was disoriented, thinking I was at the clinic. Then I remembered where I was and got out of bed. The hallway light was on, and I winced at the brightness as I picked up the phone.

"Hello," I said, my voice sounding scratchy. I cleared my throat. "This is Dr. Sunny."

"Oh, Dr. Sunny," Ragu's voice wafted through the receiver. "I'm sorry to wake you up, but I have bad news."

I couldn't believe what Ragu was telling me. The attack on Girija and my dog was heartbreaking.

"How is Girija," I asked when he paused for a breath.

"She is traumatized but not hurt. We are back at the clinic."

Poor Girija. It turned out Callum was the hero in this story. I really didn't want to think of his heroism at the moment.

"Karu is at the vet and is going to be alright," Ragu said.

"Can I go see Karu," I asked. "Is she at Dr. Veena's?"

"Yes. The clinic is closed for the night. Scot Sir stayed until he knew Karu was going to be alright. He said you can visit her tomorrow."

I thanked him and hung up. Of course, now I couldn't go back to sleep. I sat on the bed, waiting for dawn.

CHAPTER FORTY-SEVEN
SHANTA HAS A PLAN FOR CALLUM

Callum woke up to the sound of someone banging on the front door. He slipped on his bathrobe and found the hallway crowded with people.

"Quiet down, here he is," he heard someone shouting.

Shanta pushed her way to stand in front of him.

"Scot Sir," she began.

"What's going on?" Callum interrupted. "Isn't it a bit early to have a party?"

He meant it as a joke, but Shanta shook her head with a grave look on her face.

"These people are here to help you with your problem."

At Callum's bewildered expression, Shanta explained the plan.

"Scot Sir," she explained patiently. "You want to win back the doctor, and these villagers are here to help."

Ari stepped up and stood next to Shanta.

"Scot Sir," he said. "We have come up with a possible solution to your problem. You see, we have a custom in our village where the groom and his family go to the bride's house and ask for her hand in the marriage. They bring gifts to entice the bride and her family."

Callum was still looking lost, so Shanta took him by his elbow.

"Come, Scot Sir," she said, leading him to the living room. "Sit down and have a cup of tea to clear your mind."

She poured him a cup of strong black tea and added a splash of milk. He sipped on the hot drink, feeling the caffeine do its job.

"Now, Shanta, please explain what is going on?" he asked.

"It's like this, Scot Sir," Ari sat beside him. "We go and ask for the Doctor's hand in marriage."

Callum stood up so quickly that the dining chair toppled over. Ari bent down to pick it up.

"Whoa," Callum held up his hands. "No way am I going to ask for her hand in marriage in front of the entire village," he said. "Not going to happen."

Everyone began to talk at once.

"Everyone be quiet," Shanta's voice cut through the cacophony. "Thank you for coming up with a plan and offering to help Scot Sir. But now, I need you to leave so I can talk to Scot Sir alone."

Shanta waited for the crowd to leave the room before speaking.

"You have to listen to me, Scot sir," she said. "This is the only way you can get Dr. Sunny's attention. Once you have her attention, you can talk to her. You don't have to do it in front of everyone. You can pull her aside."

Callum shook his head and said, "No. I can't do it."

Shanta sat beside him and asked, "What is the other alternative? Wait for her to talk to you?"

Callum didn't say anything for a long moment.

"What exactly does this entail?" he finally asked.

"It is nothing, Scot sir," Shanta assured him. "We'll take care of all the details. You just show up and walk with us to her house."

She added, "You will need to give her a goat or cow."

"What?"

"It is the custom," she said. "It shows you are serious about her."

"I don't believe this," he muttered. "And where would I get a goat or cow?"

"Leave it to me," Shanta said.

"Of course, you are just like Jeeves," Callum said.

"Jeeves? Who is this person? Someone from your family?"

"Never mind," Callum said.

A few hours later, Callum was amazed to see a fine-looking brown heifer on his front lawn. She had white patches on her forehead and was calmly chewing on his flower beds.

"So, now you have a gift," Shanta said triumphantly. "What do you think?"

Callum stroked his chin. "She looks like a fine animal. Does she have a name?"

"No, you can name her later."

"Perhaps I'll let Sunny name her," he said.

"It's settled then," Shanta said happily. "We leave at dawn on Wednesday."

Callum felt his life was spinning out of control. There was nothing to do except go along with this mad scheme.

CHAPTER FORTY-EIGHT

SUNNY AND KARU

The house was still dark when I crept out of the bedroom. I couldn't wait any longer to see how Karu was doing. I was trying to slip out the front door when I heard someone clearing their throat behind me.

"Ahem…where do you think you are going?" It was my twin, Appu.

I turned and ran into his arms.

"Appu, when did you get here?"

"I took an early morning flight, and the taxi just dropped me off," he said.

"I want to go see Karu, my dog. She's been hurt and is at the vet," I muttered into his chest.

"Okay, I'll drive," he said. "Where are we going? And when did you get a dog?"

"Lower Mahagiri," I said. "The vet is an old friend. I'll explain everything on our way."

A few minutes later, we were on our way to Lower Mahagiri. The eastern sky was a deep purple with silver streaks. Sunrise was a warm promise on the distant horizon.

"Thanks for coming with me," I said to Appu.

He shook his head and asked, "What happened? I only got bits and pieces of the story."

I told him what I knew.

"That Callum saved the day," he said.

I said nothing and was glad when we pulled into the vet clinic parking lot. The office was closed, and when I looked at my watch, I saw it was barely five in the morning.

"Let's go get a cup of tea," Appu said. "Woodlands Hotel should be open, and we can return in an hour or so."

Once we finished our hot drinks, I was ready to go to the clinic, and this time, I knocked on the door, not caring it was still barely daybreak.

"Coming, coming," a voice called out from inside.

Veena, the vet, pulled open the door and looked at us with a scowl.

"This better be an emergency," she started to say, and then she recognized me.

"Dr. Sunny," she pulled me in for a tight hug. "Come in. Come in."

She led us into the back of the clinic.

"Your dog is doing fine. She had a restful night and is drinking water."

Poor Karu looked so small in the holding cell (a cage), but she tried to sit up when she heard my voice.

I stroked her head. "Karu, it's all right. You're going to be fine. What a brave dog you are."

She licked my fingers, and I felt tears prickling my eyelids.

"She could use another day in the clinic," the vet said. "Then I can make sure she has no infection or internal injuries. Is that okay with you, Dr. Sunny?"

I wiped my eyes and nodded.

Appu came to stand next to me, "She looks like she's going to be fine, Sunny," he said, hugging me.

Again, I nodded.

Appu then introduced himself to Veena, and I watched them shake hands.

"I'll call you with an update tonight," Veena promised.

"Thanks, Dr. Veena," I said.

"You are welcome, Dr. Sunny," she said with a smile.

As we walked out of the clinic, I shoved my elbow into Appu's chest.

"Stop making googly eyes at the vet," I teased him.

He stared down at me and asked, "Googly eyes? What are you talking about?"

"You can't fool me, Appu brother," I said, feeling lightheaded. "You were staring at Veena. Admit it, you thought she was good-looking."

He shook his head and was about to say something, but I started to laugh.

"Now, I know you are going mad," he muttered.

"I was just teasing you," I said. "And she is nice looking."

"Yes, she is," he admitted as we approached the government hospital.

Meena and her baby were both doing well. They were expecting to go home in a day or two.

"*Kutty*," my mother said. "Meena is going to be fine. You should not neglect your other patients. Go to the clinic. I'm sure Ragu and Girija will be glad to see you."

I reluctantly agreed, and later that day, Appu drove me to the clinic, where I found Girija and Ragu waiting for me.

"Oh, Dr. Sunny," Girija hugged me so tightly that I had difficulty catching my breath. "I'm so glad to see you."

I pulled away and looked at her. She had a bandage on her neck.

"Are you alright? How's the cut on your neck?"

She shook her head and wiped tears from her face.

"I'm alright. It's just a small nick. I don't know what would have happened if Scot sir hadn't come," she said. "I owe my life to him."

CHAPTER FORTY-NINE

IT TAKES A VILLAGE

Callum had been teasing when he called Shanta 'Jeeves'; however, the woman proved to be a super organizer. She told him that the wedding procession would take place in two days. Bhadra had arrived late in the day and was full of unsolicited advice.

"It is an auspicious day," Bhadra said. "We'll take you from Ari's house to the clinic, and with all of us supporting you, you will ask for Dr Sunny's hand in marriage."

Callum again felt he was losing control of his life and said, "I don't like the idea of doing this in front of everyone. What if she says no?"

"She won't say no," Bhadra laughed. "It is an auspicious day."

She added with a teasing look, "The cow will change her mind in any case."

Callum didn't know whether she was serious or not. There was no arguing with Shanta and Bhadra. He had to hope this was the best way to win back Sunny. He needed room to breathe, so he told the ladies he was going to Lower Mahagiri to see how Karu was doing. He was glad to get out of the house and away from the women.

He arrived at the vet clinic to find the doctor getting ready to leave on an emergency. She let him in, and he was glad to see Karu looking well. She was sitting up and alert.

"Hey, lassie, how are you doing?" he gently stroked her soft head. "Looks like you'll be ready to go home soon."

"About that," the vet spoke up behind him. He stood up and turned to face her.

"The dog is ready to go home. I have an emergency call in the nearby village and was wondering if you could take Karu to Dr. Sunny's clinic?"

Callum didn't hesitate for a moment.

"Of course," he said.

Soon, Karu was tucked between several blankets and towels on the jeep floor. He had to drive slowly; it was past midnight when he pulled up into the meadow. The clinic was dark. He turned and looked at the dog.

"So, Karu, how about you spend the night at my house? And we'll see the good doctor first thing tomorrow morning."

Karu wagged her tail, and Callum turned the jeep around and headed toward his estate. He carried the dog into his house and found Bhadra and Shanta waiting for him.

"Scot Sir," Shanta said. "Where have you been? The priest was here to go over the plans for tomorrow morning."

Her voice trailed off when she saw the bundle in his arms.

"How did you get Dr. Sunny's dog?" she asked.

Callum gently placed the dog on the rug in front of the fire. "I went to the vet clinic to see how Karu was doing, and the vet asked if I could take her home because she had an emergency. I agreed, and here she is."

"Why didn't you take the dog to the Sunshine Clinic?" Bhadra asked.

"I went there, but it was so late and…."

Bhadra interrupted him. "This is perfect. You can include Karu as part of your gift. Along with the cow."

Callum stared at the woman smiling at him. He shook his head.

"I give up," he said, standing up. "You two are way ahead of me in the scheming department."

Shanta wanted Callum to get some rest, but he insisted on sleeping on a pile of blankets right next to Karu.

It seemed like he had just fallen asleep when Shanta was shaking him awake.

"Scot Sir, you need to take a bath and put on some clean clothes," she said.

Soon, he was climbing into the jeep with Ragu, Shanta, and Bhadra. Callum helped Karu into the jeep. He hugged the warm animal and wondered what would happen in the next few hours. Either he would convince Sunny to marry him, or he'd make a fool of himself in front of the entire village. Moving back to the Highlands seemed a definite possibility.

CHAPTER FIFTY
SUNNY GETS A PROPOSAL

It had been a horrendously busy evening. By the time I ushered out the last patient, it was late. I called Veena to ask about Karu, but she wasn't answering her phone. Perhaps she was out on a call. I would try again first thing in the morning. For once, I fell asleep without taking my evening bath.

"Dr. Sunny, wake up," Girija was shaking me awake.

I was bleary-eyed, and my mouth was dry.

"What?" I muttered. "Is there a patient?"

"Not exactly," Girija said, looking nervous and excited. "You need to get dressed and come outside."

"I'll just put on my robe," I said, reaching for a comfortable bathrobe.

"No, no," Girija insisted. "You need to get dressed."

I grumbled as I pulled on a pair of jeans and a sweater.

"You might want to wash your face and comb your hair," Girija said, wringing her hands.

"What is going on?" I asked as I splashed cold water on my face.

I gathered up my hair into a knot on top of my head.

"I'm ready," I said.

Girija looked at me and shook her head.

I was about to enter the clinic when she pulled me toward the living room instead. She opened the front door, and we stepped out onto the porch. The sun was just rising in the east, and the sky was a silver grey. I heard the sound of beating drums and saw the strangest sight. A large group of villagers were heading toward the clinic. A few held makeshift tiki-type torches. I couldn't make out who was in this odd procession. I turned to Girija with a questioning look. She patted my arm. That's when I felt someone else on my other side.

"Amma," I cried out. "What are you doing here?"

"Sunny," my sister Meena said from the other side.

"Meena, should you be out of bed?" I asked. "And why is everyone here?

"It's okay," she said with a smile. "I'm just standing here, not lifting bags of rice."

"Where's the baby?" I asked, still confused.

"Right here," it was Raj with a bundle in his arms.

I bent over the sweet face.

"You are looking at young Mac," Meena said in my ear.

"Oh, that is a wonderful name for him," I said.

"Thangam," my mother tugged my arm to get my attention. "Look."

I turned, and my mouth dropped in astonishment. Callum led the procession, holding a rope with a cow on the end of it. A cow? For a moment, I thought I was having a very realistic dream. Callum stopped in front of us. I could now see he was wearing a dhoti cloth around his waist, and he was bare-chested with a white cloth draped around his shoulders. He had an impressive-looking but rather precarious turban wrapped around his head. There was a smear of red powder on his fore-head. He seemed thoroughly uncomfortable, and for a moment,

I thought I would burst into laughter. Luckily, before I could giggle, Ari stepped forward with a solemn expression on his face.

"Little Mother," he greeted us, "Dr. Sunny. I represent the groom. He is a good man. Scot Sir, I mean, Mr. Callum has come to ask your hand in marriage."

I was flabbergasted and speechless, even if I wanted to say something. Bhadra stepped from my mother's side. Was everyone in on this?

"What does the groom have to offer?" she asked Ari.

Ari gestured to Callum, who walked up with the cow, who wasn't in a cooperating mood.

"We have a cow," Ari said. He dug his elbow into Callum's side, and I could see him wince.

"Yes," Callum sounded hoarse. He cleared his throat. "Yes, I have this valuable cow and, of course, my house and estate."

Bhadra nodded and said approvingly, "That is a good offer. So, Dr. Sunny, what do you have to say?"

"Me?" I asked in a whisper. I cleared my throat and looked down at Callum, who was staring at me anxiously.

My mother turned to me so that I was facing her. She held my face in her hands and stared into my eyes.

"*Kutty*, do you love this man? And do you want to spend the rest of your life with him?"

I nodded even though it was hard, with my mother holding so tightly to my head.

"Then what is your answer?" she asked.

I didn't know what to say when I happened to glance at Callum, who looked adorable in his ridiculous outfit. Of course, I loved him. How could I not? He was willing to make a fool of himself in front of the entire village. I knew my answer.

"Callum," I called out.

He came closer, and I stepped down to meet him.

"We still have a lot to discuss," I said, staring into his blue eyes. "You have some explaining to do," I added sternly.

He nodded and gulped nervously. "I've been trying to talk to you. Ella means nothing to me," he began to say.

I stopped him. "Later," I whispered and walked up to the porch.

"Wait," Callum said. "There is one more gift."

I couldn't believe it as Karu slipped away from Ragu and ran toward me. She jumped into my arms, and I sat down to hug her. I felt tears running down my cheeks, and as I held her, all my fears melted away. I only had love in my heart.

I stood up and glanced at the family and friends standing behind me, and then I looked at Callum and said, "Yes, I will marry him."

The crowd erupted in cheers, and the drummers started beating a jubilant rhythm.

"Sunny," he started to say, but Bhadra didn't waste any time and pulled Callum toward me. She took his hand and placed it in mine.

"You are meant for each other," the healer said. "This is not a prophecy; it is the truth."

As Callum turned to face me, we both knew Bhadra was right.

THE END

RECIPES
RECIPE INDEX

Note: These recipes have been tested by friends and family and have not been tested in a professional kitchen.

ACCIDENTAL DELICIOUS SOUP (MAKES 2 SERVINGS)

WHEN I ADDED SOME LEFTOVER HOMEMADE HUMMUS TO A POT of potato kale soup, I accidentally created a delicious and creamy dish. Now, I make sure I have some extra hummus on hand to add to vegetable soups and sauces to give them a tangy taste. This is a very forgiving soup. You can play around with the ingredients without affecting the final quality.

Ingredients

- 2 large potatoes, rinsed and chopped
- 1 bunch kale, rinsed, stems removed and chopped
- 2-4 cups of water
- 1 medium onion, diced
- 2 cloves garlic, minced
- 1 bay leaf
- 2 tablespoons olive oil
- 2 tablespoons nutritional yeast (optional)
- ½ cup prepared hummus, any flavor
- Salt and pepper
- Fresh herbs (I used parsley and dill)

Instructions

Heat the oil in a large pot. Add onions and sauté until translucent, about 5 minutes. Add bay leaf, garlic and nutritional yeast, if using, and mix thoroughly.

Add chopped potatoes and 2 cups of water. Bring to a boil and simmer until potatoes are parboiled. Add chopped kale and cook for 5 minutes until the greens are tender. Turn off heat and add hummus. Taste and add more salt if necessary. Add more water if the soup is too thick. Garnish with chopped herbs.

BONDA RECIPE (MAKES ABOUT 8 BONDAS)

BONDAS ARE AN ADDICTIVE SNACK. THESE WERE A RARE TREAT for us since my mother didn't always approve of deep-fried foods.

Ingredients

Filling:

- 4 medium potatoes, boiled, peeled and mashed
- 1 red or white onion finely chopped
- 1 tablespoon vegetable oil
- ½ teaspoon red chili powder
- 1 teaspoon. freshly grated ginger
- 1 teaspoon mustard seeds
- 1 teaspoon. cumin seeds
- ¼ teaspoon asafetida or hing (optional)
- 1 teaspoon turmeric powder
- 1 heaping teaspoon of garam masala powder
- 1-2 teaspoons salt (or to taste)
- Fresh cilantro leaves, chopped (optional)

Batter:

- 🐾 1 cup besan or chickpea flour
- 🐾 ¼ teaspoon baking soda (optional)
- 🐾 ¼ teaspoon turmeric
- 🐾 ½ teaspoon salt
- 🐾 Water as needed
- 🐾 Oil for deep frying

Instructions

Prepare the filling:

Heat oil in a pan, add mustard seeds. Cover pan and let the seeds splutter and pop. Once the popping has stopped add cumin seeds, onions and hing. Stir and cook until onions are soft and translucent. Add ginger, turmeric, red chili powder, salt and garam masala. Mix well. Add mashed potatoes and combine everything. Stir in chopped cilantro leaves. Remove potato mixture from heat and set aside.

Prepare the batter:

Mix the chickpea flour, salt, baking soda (if using) and turmeric. Gradually add water to form a thick batter without any lumps. Set it aside.

Cook the Bondas:

Heat oil in a deep pan. While the oil is heating prepare the bondas. Take about a tablespoon of the potato filling and shape into a ball. Do this with the rest of the potato filling. Set the bondas aside.

When the oil is hot, dip each bonda in the batter, making sure it is fully coated. Fry in batches until golden brown and crispy.

Remove bondas from the oil with a slotted spoon and place on a tray or cookie sheet lined with paper towels.

Serve bondas with chutney and hot chai.

CARDAMOM SHORTBREAD COOKIES (MAKES ABOUT 15 COOKIES OR BARS)

THESE MELT-IN-YOUR MOUTH COOKIES ARE BASED ON A LAND O Lakes Shortbread Bar recipe. The addition of cardamom and expresso powders lends an exotic and delicious flavor to these buttery cookies..

Ingredients

- ½ cup unsalted butter, softened to room temperature
- ¼ cup sugar
- 1 cup all-purpose flour
- 2 tablespoons cornstarch
- ¼ teaspoon salt
- 2 teaspoons ground cardamom powder
- 1 teaspoon expresso powder

Instructions

Preheat oven to 350 degrees.

Combine flour, cornstarch, salt, cardamom powder and expresso powder. Set it aside. Beat the butter and sugar until creamy. Add ¼ cup of the flour mixture at a time to the butter and beat on low speed. Beat until all the flour is well incorporated.

Press the dough into an ungreased 8 or 9-inch pan and bake for 18 to 20 minutes. Cool for 5 minutes and cut into bars.

NOTE: The dough can also be rolled into a 2-inch log and chilled for 30 minutes. Once chilled, the dough can be cut into cookies and baked. Check after 15 minutes.

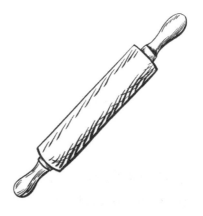

CARROT-GINGER SOUP
(SERVES 2)

GINGER ADDS A SUBTLE WARMTH TO THIS SOUP. TRY THIS SOUP with a grilled cheese sandwich.

Ingredients

- 4 cups chopped carrots
- 2 tablespoons vegetable oil
- 1 large white or yellow onion, diced
- 2 cloves garlic
- 1 bay leaf
- 2 to 3 cups water or vegetable stock
- 1-2 teaspoons salt (depending on whether you use stock or water)
- 1 heaping tablespoon freshly grated ginger
- 1-2 tablespoons nutritional yeast (optional)
- ¾ cup coconut milk, about half a can
- Fresh dill for garnish

Instructions

In a large soup pot or Dutch oven, heat the oil. Add onions and sauté until soft. Add bay leaf, garlic and ginger. Mix well. Add optional nutritional yeast and chopped carrots. Pour in the water or vegetable stock and 1 teaspoon salt. Bring to a boil and then simmer for 20 minutes until carrots are soft and falling apart.

Use an immersion blender and blend to desired consistency. Stir in coconut milk. Sprinkle with fresh dill and serve with a dollop of yogurt.

CARROTS WITH DILL BUTTER
(SERVES 2)

Roasting the carrots brings out their natural sweetness. Dill, butter and curry seasoning adds a new dimension to this simple dish.

Ingredients

- 8 or 9 carrots, washed and cut into 3-inch pieces
- 1 tablespoon olive oil
- ¾ teaspoon sea salt
- ½ to 1 teaspoon curry powder, Harissa or other seasoning blend (optional)
- 1 clove garlic, coarsely crushed
- 2 tablespoons salted butter
- 1/3 cup finely chopped fresh dill

Instructions

Preheat oven to 400 degrees. Toss the carrots with olive oil, sea salt and seasoning blend. Spread on parchment-lined cookie sheet and roast for 20 minutes. Check after 15 minutes and stir the carrots.

Meanwhile, prepare the dill butter. Melt butter in a small saucepan and add crushed garlic. Once the butter starts to bubble, remove from heat. Let the butter cool for 5 minutes. Remove garlic bits and stir in chopped dill. Toss the roasted carrots in the dill butter just before serving.

GARLIC SAUCE
(MAKES 1 CUP)

Roasting the garlic lends a sweet and caramelized depth to this versatile sauce. Use it as sandwich spread or a dip for raw vegetables.

Ingredients

- 1 cup plain yogurt (any type, including coconut yogurt is fine)
- 2-3 tablespoons runny tahini
- 1 head of roasted garlic
- 1 tablespoon fresh lemon or lime juice
- Salt and pepper to taste

Instructions

First roast the garlic. Preheat oven to 400 degrees. Cut off the top of the garlic to expose the cloves. Wrap the head of garlic in tin foil and roast for about 40 minutes. Cool.

Combine yogurt and tahini in a bowl. Squeeze the roasted garlic cloves and mash them. Add the roasted garlic paste to the yogurt. Add lemon juice. Mix well. Season with salt and pepper as desired.

GINGER TEA WITH CHAI SPICES
(MAKES ONE CUP OF TEA)

THIS SOOTHING TEA WITH WARM SPICES IS THE PERFECT REMEDY for a scratchy throat.

Ingredients

- 🏵 1 piece of ginger root (two inches) peeled and sliced
- 🏵 2 cups cold water
- 🏵 3 whole green cardamom pods
- 🏵 2 whole cloves
- 🏵 2-4 black peppercorns
- 🏵 Honey (optional)
- 🏵 Milk (optional)

Instructions

Bring the water to boil in a small pot with a lid. Add all the spices and bring to a boil. Reduce heat, cover the pot, and let the tea simmer for 10 minutes. Strain the hot tea and add optional milk and sweetener.

INDIAN-STYLE STIR FRY VEGETABLES
(SERVES 2 AS A SIDE DISH)

COOKING THE VEGETABLES QUICKLY OVER HIGH HEAT ENSURES everything stays crunchy and delicious.

Ingredients

- 2 cups chopped vegetables (carrots, cabbage, green beans or cauliflower)
- 1 onion, sliced
- 1 bell pepper, diced (any color)
- 1 green chili, chopped (optional)
- 2 garlic cloves, minced
- 1 piece of fresh ginger (about an inch long), peeled and grated
- 2 tablespoons vegetable oil
- 1 teaspoon mustard seeds
- 1 teaspoon cumin seeds
- 1 sprig curry leaves (optional)
- 1 teaspoon turmeric powder
- ½ to 1 teaspoon salt (or to taste)
- 1 to 2 teaspoons ghee for drizzling (optional)
- Fresh coriander leaves
- Lemon wedges for serving

Instructions

Heat oil in a large saucepan with lid. Add mustard seeds and let them splutter. Immediately, add cumin seeds, onion, chili and bell pepper. Cook for about 5 minutes. Add turmeric, ginger, curry leaves, and garlic. Cook for another 2 minutes. Add chopped vegetables. Sprinkle with ½ teaspoon salt.

Stir-fry until the vegetables are tender, but not too soft. Add more salt if needed. Garnish with fresh coriander leaves and ghee.

KANGEE OR RICE GRUEL
(MAKES ABOUT A CUP)

KANGEE WAS MY MOTHER'S ANSWER TO EVERY AILMENT FROM an upset tummy to menstrual cramps. The easy-to-digest gruel makes a light meal, even if you are not ill. My mother used to break the rice down using her hands (and somehow that made the *kangee* taste even better). Traditionally, *kangee* is made from white, parboiled rice (Mahatma rice) but for a healthier option, try short-grained brown rice. NOTE: Brown rice will take longer to cook.

Ingredients

- ½ cup white rice
- 1 ¼ cup cold water
- Optional additions: salt, fresh ground pepper, a spoonful of ghee, bits of raw onion, mango or lime pickle

Instructions

Rinse rice according to package directions. Bring water to boil and add rinsed rice. Turn down heat and simmer for 20 minutes. Test to make sure the rice is well cooked. Remove from heat and cool for a few minutes. Using a potato masher or your hands, break down the rice until it is mostly mashed. Add more water if you'd like a thin *kangee* gruel. Add salt and any of the optional addons.

LAVENDAR SHORTBREAD COOKIES
(MAKES ABOUT 15 COOKIES OR BARS)

THE ADDITION OF DRIED LAVENDER BUDS GIVES THESE BUTTERY cookies a floral flavor. They are a perfect snack with hot chai.

Ingredients

- ½ cup unsalted butter, softened
- ¼ cup sugar
- 1 cup all-purpose flour
- 2 tablespoons cornstarch
- 1 tablespoon culinary lavender buds

Instructions

Preheat oven to 350 degrees.

Combine the butter and sugar in a bowl. Beat at medium speed until creamy. Gradually add flour, cornstarch and salt. Beat until well mixed.

Press into an ungreased 8-inch square pan. Bake 18-20 minutes until the edges are golden brown. Cut into bars. Cool completely before removing from the pan.

> NOTE: The dough can also be rolled into a 2-inch log and chilled for 30 minutes. Once chilled, the dough can be cut into cookies and baked. Check after 15 minutes.

LEMON RASAM WITH KALE
(SERVES 2 AS A SIDE DISH)

THE ADDITION OF KALE TO A TRADITIONAL RASAM ADDS A BURST of color and nutrition. My mother never tasted this version but I'm sure she would approve.

Ingredients

- ½ cup red lentils, rinsed
- 3-4 cups water
- 1 small bunch kale, washed and chopped, stems discarded
- 1 medium tomato, diced
- 2 garlic cloves, minced
- 1 tablespoon ghee
- 1 teaspoon turmeric powder
- 1 teaspoon cumin seeds
- 1 teaspoon cumin powder
- A pinch of Hing
- Curry leaves
- Juice from 1 lemon, adjust according to taste
- 1 teaspoon salt
- Freshly ground pepper to taste
- Chopped cilantro leaves for garnish

Instructions

Heat ghee in a saucepan. Add cumin seeds, turmeric and hing. Add tomato and cumin powder. Once the spices are coated in ghee, add rinsed lentils and water. Bring to a boil. Add salt. Let the lentils boil for about 10 minutes, covered. Add chopped kale and cook for another 10-15 minutes until the lentils are well done. Remove from heat, add lemon juice and curry leaves. Serve topped with chopped cilantro leaves and freshly ground pepper.

The broth should be tangy and flavorful. Serve with rice.

POTATO AND GREEN BEAN WITH COCONUT AND MUSTARD SEEDS (SERVES 2 AS A SIDE DISH)

Coconut and mustard seeds give this dish a nutty flavor. Any combination of vegetables would work in this recipe.

Ingredients

- 2 medium potatoes, rinsed and cut into chunks
- 1 cup green beans, cut into 1-inch pieces.
- 1 onion, diced
- 1 large tomato, chopped
- ½ cup fresh grated coconut (see note)
- 1 green chili, slit and left whole
- I tablespoon ginger, grated
- 1 teaspoon mustard seeds
- 1 sprig curry leaves
- ½ teaspoon each of turmeric and cumin powder
- 1 teaspoon coriander powder
- ¼ teaspoon red chili powder (optional)
- 1 teaspoon salt (or to taste)
- Fresh cilantro leaves for garnish

Instructions

Heat oil in a saucepan with lid over medium heat. Add the mustard seeds and let them to splutter and pop. When the popping stops, immediately add onions and sauté until they are soft. Add ginger, garlic, green chili and curry leaves. Sauté for a minute or so. Add the spice powders and then the chopped tomato. Cook until the tomato is soft. Add vegetables and salt. Cover and cook the vegetables. Stir every few minutes to make sure they don't stick. If needed, add a tablespoon or more water. Stir in fresh coconut. Adjust salt as needed. Garnish with cilantro leaves. Serve with roti or rice.

Note: Fresh, grated coconut is available in the freezer section of Indian grocery stores. Desiccated coconut can be used if fresh coconut is not available.

ROTI ROLLS: (MAKES ABOUT 6-8 ROTI ROLLS)

THESE SNACKS ARE A MUST IF YOU ARE TRAVELING IN INDIA. THE taste of homemade rotis cannot be beat but you can also use wheat tortillas.

Ingredients

For the Roti:

- 1 cup whole wheat flour
- Warm water as needed
- ½ teaspoon salt
- Ghee for cooking the rotis

For the Filling:

- 1 cup cooked vegetables such as potatoes, cauliflower or sweet peas
- 2 tablespoons vegetable oil
- 1 medium onion, sliced
- 1 tablespoon ginger, grated
- 1 teaspoon turmeric powder
- 1 teaspoon curry or garam masala powder (optional)
- 1 teaspoon cumin seeds
- 1 green chili, chopped
- 1 teaspoon salt (or to taste)

- 1 tablespoon lime or lemon juice
- Fresh cilantro for garnish

Instructions

<u>Rotis:</u>

Combine the flour and salt in a bowl. Gradually add warm water to form a soft dough. Knead for about 5 minutes until smooth. Set it aside and let it rest for 30 minutes or more. Make the filling as the dough rests.

Divide the dough into small balls (you will have about 8). Roll each one out into a thin, round roti. Don't worry if the shape is not perfect.

Heat a skillet and place a roti on the hot surface. Cook each side for 1 to 2 minutes. Brush with melted ghee or oil. Wrap the cooked rotis in a clean kitchen towel.

<u>Filling:</u>

Heat oil in a saucepan and add cumin seeds and onions. Sauté the onions until soft and then add turmeric, ginger, chili, and garam masala. Add salt and cooked vegetables. Mix until the spices and vegetables are well combined. Add lemon juice and cilantro leaves. Add more salt or lemon juice if needed.

Place a generous portion of the filling in each roti and roll the roti tightly around the filling. Wrap in wax paper or tin foil.

Roti rolls can be served with chutney dipping sauce. Adding a bit of tamarind or mango chutney to the roti before rolling will give the rotis a savory flavor.

SAUTÉED BEETS
(MAKES 2 SERVINGS)

SERVE THESE BEETS WITH RICE OR ROLL THEM UP IN ROTIS WITH a bit of spicy chutney or yogurt.

Ingredients

- 3 to 4 medium beets, peeled and sliced
- 2 tablespoons coconut oil
- 2 cloves of garlic, peeled and minced
- 1 teaspoon mustard seeds
- 2 teaspoons urid dal (split black gram)
- 1 dried chili, cut into bits
- Curry leaves
- ½ teaspoon turmeric powder
- 1 teaspoon salt (or to taste)

Instructions

Heat oil in a saucepan with lid. Add mustard seeds and let them splutter and pop. Immediately add urid dal, chili bits and curry leaves. Sauté until the dal is golden brown. Add garlic and turmeric powder. Sauté for a minute and then add chopped beets and salt. Cover and cook for 10-12 minutes until the beets are tender.

Serve the beets with rotis. Beets are delicious rolled up in a roti.

TURMERIC MILK (MAKES ONE SOOTHING CUP)

Turmeric milk is considered a "safe" food for toddlers and young children. Whole milk is warmed with turmeric and pepper and sweetened with honey. My mother, like the character Little Mother in my books, owned several cows and milk was a natural part of our diet. Almond milk or oat milk can be easily substituted in this recipe to make it vegan.

Ingredients

- 1 cup milk of your choice
- ¼ to ½ teaspoon. turmeric powder
- ¼ teaspoon ground black pepper
- 1 teaspoon honey
- ½ teaspoon dried ginger (optional)
- ¼ teaspoon. cardamom powder (optional)

Instructions

Heat milk in a saucepan until is just about to boil, remove from heat and add turmeric and black pepper. Add any of the optional spices at this time. Stir in honey.

ATTRIBUTIONS FOR ILLUSTRATIONS

<a href="https://www.freepik.com/free-vector/coffee-cup-draw-dish-illustration-isolated_88801133.htm#position=1">Image by djvstock</a> on Freepik

<a href="https://www.freepik.com/free-vector/kitchen-utensils-vector-hand-drawn-rustic-wooden-kitchenware-set-spoon-dotted-spoon-spatula_143999706.htm#position=4">Image by user15245033 on Freepik</a>

<a href="https://www.freepik.com/free-vector/five-hand-drawn-carrots-vector_16174113.htm#position=5">Image by rawpixel.com on Freepik</a>

<a href="https://www.freepik.com/free-vector/onion-illustration-vector-design-silhouette_27172380.htm#position=8">Image by logturnal on Freepik</a>

<a href="https://www.freepik.com/free-vector/hand-drawn-fresh-bell-pepper_16263431.htm#position=10">Image by rawpixel.com on Freepik</a>

<a href="https://www.freepik.com/free-vector/vector-hand-drawn-icon-kitchen-dough-roller-isolated-white-background_20623046.htm#position=11">Image by user15245033 on Freepik</a>

<a href="https://www.freepik.com/free-vector/vector-hand-drawn-icon-plant-pot-isolated-white-background_20623042.htm#position=12">Image by user15245033 on Freepik</a>

<a href="https://www.freepik.com/free-vector/hand-drawn-fresh-tomatoes_14723607.htm">Image by rawpixel.com</a> on Freepik

<a href="https://www.freepik.com/free-vector/hand-drawn-jalapeno-drawing-illustration_57430699.htm#position=1">Image by freepik</a>

ACKNOWLEDGMENTS

POWERFUL WOMEN IN MY FAMILY CONTINUE TO INSPIRE ME.

My great-grandmother, Chippu Kunchiammal, my grand-mother, Muthu Kunchiammal, my great-aunty Ammalu Kun-chiammal, and my mother, Leela Sadasivan, were exceptional women who have profoundly influenced my writing.

My aunty Christine shared her love of writing, reading (espe-cially southern literature), and decadent chocolate desserts. I am a better writer and baker because of her.

My uncle Easwaran shared his passion for English literature. He also taught me the importance of family and deepened my appreciation of Indian culture and traditions. His wisdom con-tinues to guide me.

Behind-the-scene helpers: Alan Klein, Cindy Segur, Alli Klein, and Marg Gilks of Scripta Word Services.

A big welcome to the latest member of our family, Lawson Finn Klein.

Finally, a huge thank you to all my readers for supporting my literary efforts through the years.

ABOUT THE AUTHOR
MEERA EKKANATH KLEIN
AN AWARD-WINNING AUTHOR

MEERA EKKANATH KLEIN IS THE AUTHOR OF A SERIES OF NOV-els set in south India. Her books combine her love of cooking and writing. *Sunshine Clinic: A Novel with Recipes* is the third book in the series. Her two previous novels are: *My Mother's Kitchen* and *Seeing Ceremony*.

Klein's short stories, feature articles and poems have been published in online and print magazines. She is also a reviewer for the *New York Journal of Books*. She lives in California with her husband and has two grown sons with families of their own.

Thank you for choosing to read my book. If you enjoyed the story, please take a moment to write a short review.
Reviews help get the word out about the book and encourage other readers to check out my book.
In appreciation,
Meera Klein

US   CAN   UK

AUS   IN

Made in the USA
Las Vegas, NV
15 February 2025

18167613R00184